Soviet Peasants

(or: The Peasants' Art of Starving)

by Lev Timofeev

**Edited with Introduction
by Armando Pitassio and Victor Zaslavsky**

**Translated from the Russian
by Jean Alexander and Alexander Zaslavsky**

TELOS PRESS
NEW YORK

English translation © 1985 Telos Press Ltd., New York

Published originally in Russian as *Tekhnologiya chernogo rynka ili krestyanskoe iskusstvo golodat'*, © Lev Timofeev

ISBN: 0-914386-12-3

Library of Congress Catalog Number: 85-50773

Manufactured in the United States of America

Telos Press Ltd.
431 East 12th Street
New York NY 10009

Table of Contents

Introduction:

Peasants and Kolkhozes

by Armando Pitassio and Victor Zaslavsky*

The book bearing Lev Timofeev's pseudonym, written in Moscow from 1979 to 1980 by a journalist specializing in agriculture, belongs to that rarest genre of Soviet literature — social anthropology. In his book the author combines a perceptive analysis of the workings of Soviet planned agriculture with the insight of direct observation of the Soviet peasants' everyday life. He is quite at home with the most abstract and often intentionally abstruse publications of official Soviet researchers; he had access to "official use only" materials — sources inaccessible not only to Western researchers, but to many Soviet specialists as well. Timofeev knows where to look and how to read between the lines. Finally, Timofeev is a gifted analytical observer, able to perceive the gist of complex social processes amongst the travails and tribulations of flesh-and-blood Soviet kolkhozniks.

Timofeev's book speaks for itself and would appear to need no introduction. But since the author knew he would never see his work published in the USSR, he wrote it for the *samizdat* public: the Russian intellectuals with

---

*Translated from the Italian by Eleni Mahaira-Odoni and Alexander Zaslavsky.

a strong interest in the history of their country and a highly developed sense of moral responsibility both for the recent past and for the future of the Soviet Union. Accordingly, Timofeev consistently relies on the common experience of Soviet intelligentsia, on that unity of author and reader that permits the former to leave much unsaid. In addition, Timofeev altogether ignores the Western literature on the topic, although several major investigations of Soviet peasantry have been published in the West in recent years. This introduction hopes to add to Lev Timofeev's work by addressing those aspects of the problem omitted by Timofeev in his study that could help the Western reader to a deeper understanding of the history of the kolkhoz system and the current state of affairs in Soviet agriculture.

Collectivization: The Elimination of the Kulak Class.

It is impossible to understand the kolkhoz system of today without considering the collectivization of the late 1920s and early 1930s. In terms of intensity and magnitude of social transformation that period has no equal in all of Soviet history and perhaps even in all of contemporary history. It is in this period that the foundations of the Stalinist state were laid, the Stalinist state which, slightly modified, survives in the USSR to this day.

The Soviet socio-economic system of the late 1920s was a far cry from a "mixed economy" of interspersed socialist and capitalist elements. The one-party political system had full control over nationalized industry, a relatively small but highly concentrated and influential sector of the economy. As for the enormous rural sector constituting the market economy (in 1926, 82% of the population lived in the countryside), the party and state were tenuous at best. During the severe crisis of 1927-28,[1] when the one-party system itself appeared in danger, Stalin's group emerged victorious in the factional struggles within party leadership. As S. Bialer correctly notes, Stalin "achieved dominance in the party not only because of his superior organizational skills and ruthless manipulation, but because he expressed the aspirations of the dominant groups in the Soviet party."[2] Stalin proposed a radical reconstruction of Soviet society — the major thrusts being accelerated industrialization and rapid collectivization of the countryside — the famous "revolution from above." Collectivization, in turn, involved two interrelated processes: the intensification of class struggle in the countryside with the elimination of the kulaks (the wealthier peasants) as a class, and the replacement of small, individual peasant holdings by the large collective farm — the kolkhoz.

The elimination of the kulaks proved to be one of the bloodiest operations in Stalinist history. The kulaks were defined as the wealthiest farming families, but their very existence as a separate "class" was for the most part a political fiction. Indeed, whence all these rich peasants little more than ten years after a revolution whose levelling impact was still being felt in the countryside? Already the noted economist Chayanov, among other agricultural

---

1. In this connection, see M. Reiman, *La nascita dello stalinismo* (Roma: Editori Riuniti, 1980).

2. S. Bialer, *Stalin's Successors: Leadership, Stability and Change in the Soviet Union* (Cambridge: Cambridge University Press, 1980), p. 38.

economists, called attention to the demographic origins of the economic differentiation among peasants and of the social stratification of the countryside (hence the concept of "demographic stratification"[3]). The peasant economy was based on family cooperation. Consequently, the processes within the peasant family necessarily affected the development and operation of household farm. In the absence of any kind of mechanization, family cooperation was in itself a powerful production force. Moreover, officially equalized land use meant that the number of family members bore directly on the size of the land plot allotted to the family. Today, Soviet specialists on collectivization stress the importance of the demographic factor.[4] V. Danilov observes: "The 1927 census data confirm a direct and strong correlation between the number of family members and the economic power of the family unit. A poor peasant's holding (with means of production valued up to 200 rubles) was owned by a family of 2-4 persons with one or at most two workers. The average peasant

3. A.V. Chayanov, *Ocherki po ekonomike trudovogo selskogo khozyaistva* (Moskva, 1924); also his *Organizatsiya krestyanskogo khozyaistva* (Moskva, 1925); N.P. Makarov, *Krestyanskoe khozyaistvo i ego evoltsiya* (Moskva, 1920); A.N. Chelintsev, *Dinamika krestyanskogo khozyaistva* (Moskva, 1928). On the life, times and works of Aleksandr V. Chayanov, see Basile Kerblay, "A.V. Chayanov: Life, Career, Works," in D. Thorner, B. Kerblay, R.E.F. Smith, eds., *V. Chayanov on the Theory of Peasant Economy* (Homeward, Ill., 1966): and L. Certkov," A.V. Chayanov narratore," an introductory essay to A.V. Chayanov, *Viaggio di mio fratello Aleksej nel paese dell'utopia contadina* (Torino: Einaudi, 1979).

4. V.P. Danilov, *Sovetskaya dokolkhoznaya derevnya: naselenie, zemlepol'zovanie, khozyaistvo* (Moskva: Nauka, 1977); B.N. Mironov, "Sotsial'noe rassloenie russkogo krestyanstva pod uglom zreniya sotsial'noi mobil'nosti," in *Problemy agrarnoi istorii (XIX - 30-e gody XX veka)* (Minsk: Nauka, 1978).

— *serednjak* — farm, with means of production valued between 201 and 800 rubles was managed by families of 4-6 souls of whom two or three could work. Finally, in the holdings of wealthy peasants — the kulaks — the means of production were valued in excess of 800 rubles and the family was comprised of 6-9 persons and more than three workers."[5] This paragraph alone makes it quite clear that the real level of economic differentiation in the countryside at the end of the 1920s was insignificant. According to research of 1927, the wealthiest peasants owned two, sometimes three cows and up to 10 arable hectares for an average family of 7.[6] Whenever these rich peasants resorted to hired labor, they did not employ, on the average, more than one laborer per farm. In a kulak's farm the earnings came to some 240 rubles per family member, twice the countryside average. But the average salary of a country official was 297 rubles a year. As M. Lewin observed, "Soviet rural 'capitalism' barely existed. The state could curb the richer peasants at will; indeed, it did so in 1928-29, when under pressure of taxation and forced procurements this stratum shrank very substantially and rural 'capitalism' began to melt like wax."[7] So why did Stalin initiate this ruthless policy of the kulaks' physical elimination? The answer lies in the manner in which the policy was implemented.

In Western literature it is generally believed that "in the

---

5. V.P. Danilov, *op. cit.*, pp. 223-228.

6. Yu. V. Arutyunyan, *Sotsial'naya struktura sel'skogo naseleniya SSSR* (Moskva: Mysl, 1971), p. 26.

7. M. Lewin, "Society, State and Ideology during the First Five-Year Plan," in S. Fitzpatrick, ed., *Cultural Revolution in Russia, 1928-1931* (Bloomington: Indiana University Press, 1978), p. 49.

most cases, kulaks were deported or shot by urban-based cadres who were brought into the rural areas."[8] No doubt, the role of city workers and local party functionaries in effecting the "revolution from above" was quite significant. But the urban cadres alone were obviously insufficient. In fact, the expropriation of the kulaks was largely carried out with the help of the peasant masses themselves.[9] And this is hardly surprising in view of the culture and traditions of the Russian peasant *obshchina*.

Collectivization and the Traditions of the Obshchina.

For centuries the main form of Russian peasant organization was the *obshchina* or *mir* ("world" or "universe" in Russian); it therefore occupies a special place in Russian social history. Many political thinkers celebrated the *obshchina* "as the repository of the ancient democratic virtues and the innate socialistic tendencies of the Russian people, as a unique form of collective life, that, having miraculously survived through the centuries, set them apart from other, less spiritual and more grossly materialistic nations."[10] Even Marx, analyzing the possibilities of a distinct, non-capitalist process of Russian development, relied on this historically false ideal of the *obshchina*. Actually, the *obshchina* was a social institution which arose with the state's active support and functioned as a fiscal entity whose members were collectively responsible for

---

8. A. Dallin, G. Breslauer, *Political Terror in Communist Systems* (Stanford: Stanford University Press, 1970), p. 63.

9. See Roger Portal's introduction to M. Lewin. *La paysannerie et le pouvoir sovietique 1928-1930* (Paris, 1966).

10. T. Szamuely, *The Russian Tradition* (London: Secker and Warburg, 1974), pp. 46-47.

the taxes levied against the *obshchina* as a whole. The *obshchina* had ample powers: it divided tax payments among its members, made sure the peasants did not flee from the landowners (in which case taxes for others increased proportionally), it was responsible for furnishing army recruits and could also punish its lazy or criminal members, who could be exiled to Siberia without trial, exclusively upon the *obshchina*'s decision. In addition, the *obshchina* assigned to each family a land plot roughly based on the number of family members and periodically redistributed land to account for the differences in the fertility of soil. All decisions were made democratically at public assemblies. And yet, noted K. Wittfogel, this was a "beggar's democracy" — "it was an autonomous peasant community, running its own affairs with no outside interference, on democratic and egalitarian lines, wielding considerable authority — but every single one of its members was the landowner's chattel, to be bartered or sold with impunity."[11] The *obshchina* provided its members with security and protection, but stifled individual initiative: its ethics found expression in the maxim "nobody should live better than I."

Following the abolition of serfdom in 1861 and even after the revolution, the peasant *obshchina* (renamed "agricultural society") continued to function in the countryside. It went on with land redistributions in attempting to maintain equitable land use;[12] the peasant assembly even retained the right to punish its members: in the 1920s, well before collectivization, these assemblies could forcibly evict a peasant and confiscate his plot for failing

---

11. *Ibid.*, p. 47.
12. V.P. Danilov, *op. cit.*, p. 116.

to pay taxes and "defying the agricultural society."[13]

Through a policy whereby any peasant better off than others could be branded a kulak and evicted with confiscation of property, the Stalin administration appropriated the age-old traditions of the Russian *obshchina* in order to "intensify the class struggle in the countryside." In this light, collectivization emerges as the elimination of the most productive and efficient family farms and of the stablest families, endowed with the strongest work ethic and most receptive to modernization. In only five years of collectivization more than 700,000 peasant families were deported.[14] Considering the average kulak family of 7-8 souls, the victims of the kulak liquidation campaign numbered at least five million. Many kulaks were shot on the spot rather than deported; of the rest many perished en route to Siberia.

The astuteness of Stalin's plan lay in the fact that the land, house and other property of deported families became property of the newly-organized kolkhoz. Those peasants who joined the kolkhoz and consigned their land and animals to collective use became in a sense wealthier, since they became co-owners of the land and property of the evicted kulak families. Thus, aside from jibing with the ingrained traditions of the *obshchina*, this policy also provided strong material incentive for the poorer peasants to join the kolkhoz.[15] All-encompassing

13. *Ibid.* p. 103.

14. R.W. Davies, *The Industrialization of Soviet Russia*, V. I, *The Social Offensive: The Collectivization of Soviet Agriculture, 1929-1930* (Cambridge: Harvard University Press, 1980).

15. M.A. Sholokhov, *Virgin Soil Upturned* (London: Putnam, 1935); D. Atkinson, *The End of the Russian Land Commune 1905-1930* (Stanford: Stanford University Press, 1983), pp. 364-367.

collectivization that, in a few years, turned 90% of Soviet peasants into kolkhozniks could never have been effected so quickly without the liquidation of the kulaks as a class. In all, collectivization was partly voluntary, partly coerced: while many peasants were forced into the kolkhoz, others were lured into joining both by the promise of future benefits and by actual participation in the sharing of kulak possessions. As a result, by the mid 1930s, the kolkhoz, a new productive and fiscal unit, began to dominate over the traditional, small household farm in the Soviet countryside.

Theories of Collectivization.

The issue of collectivization continues to spark heated discussions among students of Soviet society. What prompted Stalin's leadership to introduce collectivization? What were the social consequences of the collectivization for Soviet peasantry and, more broadly, for Soviet society? There are essentially three "theories" on this subject.

The official Soviet version reiterates Stalin's explanation of collectivization as the revolution from above. According to this theory, collectivization represented the socialization of the countryside, the integration of agriculture into the system of central planning, and a general upgrading of agricultural productivity. The Soviet version draws succour from the uncontestable fact that, as an economic entrprise, the kolkhoz in no way contradicted the vision of higher productivity: theoretically, the kolkhoz ought to be more productive than the small peasant holdings deprived of new technology. The weakness of the Soviet theory is simple: it describes what could have happened, but never did. The immediate and persistent effects of collectivization proved to be a dramatic decline in productivity, massive slaughter of livestock and devastating famine. Soviet statistics cited by Timofeev illustrate how Stalinist collectivization transformed Soviet peasants into semi-slaves — a source of free labor for the state.

In the West, the widely accepted theory of collectivization could be termed a theory of "internal colonialism." The peasants represent a domestic colony of the Soviet state that is plundered and exploited in order to finance the creation of heavy industry:

> It was an internal colonialism mobilizing its state power against colonial tributaries in rural territories... The control center governs by using the state to impose unequal exchange through discussions governing capital allocations, prices and price controls, investments, access by visitors, taxes, tax exemptions and deductions, credit, loans, labor drafts, military conscription, rates of interest, wages, tariffs, custom duties, access to education, passports and visas, and electoral representation. Where these routine mechanisms fail, the control center uses force and violence against the remote subordinates.[16]

According to this theory, collectivization is analogous to the process of primitive accumulation as described by Marx in his analysis of the origins of capitalism. In the

---

16. A. Gouldner, "Stalin: A Study of Internal Colonialism," *Telos*, no. 34 (Winter 1977-78), p. 13.

Soviet Union this theory is indebted to the seminal writings of a well-known economist, E. Preobrazhenskii, who, as early as in the 1920s, claimed that industry could only be financed at the expense of the peasants. In his view, capital could be drained from the countryside by maintaining high prices on industrial goods and low prices on agricultural products — the notorious "scissors" principle. All of this was couched in terms of historical necessity: only thus would it be possible to industrialize a backward country enervated by war and surrounded by foes.

In recent years, the weaknesses of the internal colonialism theory have come under increasing attack from specialists who advance the so-called "revisionist theory of collectivization."[17] These specialists claim that a specific analysis of the economics of collectivization dispels the view of the countryside as a source of capital for industry. For in truth the capital moved in the opposite direction. True, "the state secured essential supplies of agricultural products at prices far below the market level. But taking collections and market sales together, the prices received by the agricultural producers increased far more rapidly than the prices of industrial goods. The terms of trade turned in favor of agriculture."[18] Moreover, collectivization annihilated the most productive segment of the peasantry and produced a real, if minor migration of skilled labor from the city to the countryside — the

---

17. J.R. Millar, "What Is Wrong With The Standard Story," in *Problems of Communism*, 25:4, 1976, pp. 50-55, 59-61; also his, "Collectivization and Its Consequences: A New Look," *Russian Review*, 41:1, 1982, pp. 60-67.

18. R.W. Davies, *op. cit.,* p. 369.

workers sent out to enforce collectivization who subsequently stayed in the countryside.

Critical of the thesis of the rural sector as a source of industrial financing, the revisionist theory explains collectivization as a purely political decision of the Stalin administration. Collectivization was a means of establishing total control of the one-party system and its bureaucratic apparatus over the agrarian sector. As already Barrington Moore pointed out, "with a strangle hold on the food supply... the peasants represented, even in their inchoate and spontaneous fashion, a distinct and independent nucleus of power, able to exercise leverage on all other aspects of policy."[19] Collectivization wiped out this economic independence and ensured the state's absolute control over the countryside. M. Lewin even questions the very concept of the "revolution from above" by arguing that collectivization was simply the culmination of the policy of administrative violence against the peasantry which began in 1927-28 following the critical food shortages in the cities.[20] In general, however, collectivization is perceived as a premeditated policy aimed at eliminating all opposition groupings within the party that leaned toward a more moderate policy.

There is little doubt that foregoing theories of collectivization are more complementary than contradictory. A complete theory of collectivization is still to be formulated. The official Soviet version sheds light on the Soviet administration's sincere efforts to rationalize agri-

19. J. Barrington Moore Jr., *Terror and Progress. USSR: Some Sources of Change and Stability in the Soviet Dictatorship* (Cambridge: Harvard University Press, 1966), p. 73.

20. M. Lewin, *La Paysannerie. . ., op. cit.*

culture and underscores the fact that collectivization could have been a viable program had it not been carried out by barbaric means in an absurdly short period of time. The kolkhoz could be an efficient productive structure had it not been for the Stalinist system of management and cruel repression that forcibly attached the peasants to the land. Such views have been expounded even in the USSR by the historian R. Medvedev in his essay on Stalinism.[21]

As for the theory of internal colonialism, however wrong its thesis of the countryside as a source of industrial financing, it still allows for the appreciation of collectivization and Stalinist industrialization as complex and interdependent processes. Collectivization made it possible to supply rapidly growing cities with foodstuffs expropriated from the kolkhoz and succeeded in forcing the peasants to work through non-economic measures. Collectivization even provided the cities and the nascent industries with manpower. Previously, the working class numbered a total of 4.5 million; after collectivization the peasants flocked to the cities *en masse*, ready for any work. In the years of collectivization alone, about 18 million peasants moved to the city, causing the "ruralization of cities."[22] As a consequence, collectivization further contributed to conditions that compelled city workers to work without holding back — hence higher productivity — despite the precipitously falling standard of living: very low wages, terrible housing and strict discipline.

---

21. R. Medvedev, *Let History Judge: The Origins and Consequences of Stalinism* (New York: Knopf, 1971).

22. M. Lewin, "Society...," *op. cit.*, pp. 47-55.

Finally, the revisionist theory of collectivization emphasizing its political aspect, focusing on the importance of the decisive victory of central planning over the market in Soviet economy. Simultaneously, collectivization reinforced the one-party system in its Stalinist incarnation. The suppression of all autonomous rural forces subordinated the countryside to the party bureaucracy apparatus. As K.E. Wädekin notes, this was an optimal operation of "establishing complete control over the peasant majority of the population."[23]

The Kolkhoz: a Mechanism of Forced Labor.

The success of the campaign for total collectivization was already evident by the mid 1930s. There were fewer than 10% of individual peasant holdings left in the country. Their resistance against joining the kolkhoz was hopeless. According to research done in late 1934, only 7.7% of the independent peasants were willing to join while, the researcher observes, "administrative measures were being applied against 26.2% of independent agricultural producers."[24] The kolkhoz dominated the countryside.

Life in the kolkhoz frustrated the expectations of those peasants who had joined voluntarily in the hope of bettering their lives. The elimination of the kulaks robbed the countryside of many productive and qualified peasants. Still more importantly, the kolkhoz proved to be the

---

23. K.E. Wadekin, *Agrarian Policies in Communist Europe. A Critical Introduction* (Totowa, N.J.: Allanheld, Osmund & Co., 1982), p. 23.

24. *Problemy istorii sovetskogo krestyanstva* (Moskva: Nauka, 1981), p. 137.

state's ideal instrument for plundering the peasants. By setting high, often impossible production quotas and by fixing minimal prices on agricultural products, the state used kolkhoz members as free labor. If the individual peasant could perhaps conceal part of his crop from the state, the kolkhoznik could not do so. The kolkhoz became a very efficient fiscal institution, similar to the peasant *obshchina* of the past. Characteristically, agricultural administrators attached to the German occupation forces of 1941-43 fully appreciated the usefulness of collective farms: "They noted that the collective farm was an admirable means to compel peasants to produce and deliver grain, and they tried to keep kolkhozy in operation in much of the territory they occupied."[25] It was precisely for this reason, explains Timofeev, that Stalin suppressed the voluntary peasant communes of the pre-collectivization era — organizations ostensibly closest to the ideals of communism — and replaced them with collective farms.

The same brutality that brought about collectivization without regard for expediency or human life also characterized the kolkhoz tax collection. The state production quotas had to be fulfilled at all costs, even if the kolkhozniks were left with noting. Here is the eloquent testimony of Boris Pasternak, a contemporary of the collectivization, who wrote the following on the kolkhoz life in those days:

> At the beginning of the thirties there was
> a movement among the writers to visit the

---

25. G. Yaney, *The Urge to Mobilize. Agrarian Reform in Russia, 1861-1930* (Urbana: University of Illinois Press, 1982), p. 550.

collective farms and gather material for books about the new countryside. I wanted to be like everybody else and also went off on a trip with the idea of writing a book. There are no words to describe what I saw there. It was such an inhuman, unimaginable misfortune, such a terrible calamity that it was on the way to becoming an abstraction, as it were — the mind could not take it in. I fell ill. For a whole year I couldn't sleep.[26]

Using Soviet statistics, Timofeev shows the horrifying level of kolkhoz exploitation in the 1930s. According to official data, a third of the collective farms paid their members next to nothing for their work, while most others paid so little that it was impossible to get by. How then did the kolkhozniks survive after collectivization? Why did they not all flee to the city? Finally, why did they continue to till the kolkhoz fields instead of retreating to a subsistence economy? To answer these question we need first to analyze two basic mechanisms of control and coercion created during Stalin's reign, mechanisms that although slightly modified continue to operate to this day. These are the passport system and the system of personal plots.

The passport system was introduced by Stalin's administration in December of 1932 and was completely in place by the mid 1930s. At the age of 16 every Soviet

---

26. O. Ivinskaja, *A Captive of Time* (Garden City, N.J.: Doubleday, 1978), p. 71. For the best Soviet author's description of the collectivization period see V.S. Grossman, *Forever Flowing* (New York: Harper and Row, 1972).

citizen must possess an internal passport. The right to stay and work in the city is conditional on this document. Kolkozniks, however, were not issued passports. The passport system attached the majority of the peasants to their collective farms and facilitated rigorous control over the migration of those peasants who somehow managed to escape the kolkhoz. Only in 1981 did the kolkhozniks finally obtain passports. But even today their mobility is severely limited: in order to reside permanently in a city, authorization (a so-called *propiska*) is necessary, and it may or may not be granted at the discretion of the city's police authorities.

Having prevented a mass exodus of the peasants from the kolkhoz and having brought the migration channels under control, the Soviet administration still had another problem to solve. Unable to flee the kolkhoz, the peasant could simply stop working there, leave the sphere of socialized production and live off his own small personal plot. To forestall this eventuality, Stalin's administration developed a series of measures, including the transfer "in perpetuity" of all lands to the kolkhoz, and the very structure of the kolkhoz — a large, collectively cultivated estate together with many small plots autonomously worked by individual kolkozniks and their families. This structure turned out to be the second important mechanism of coercion and control in the kolkhoz system.

The Personal Plots of the Kolkhozniks.

Western mass-market publications have spun an entire legend around the plots personally owned by kolkozniks. For instance, H. Smith, in his famous 1975 book, *The*

Russians, writes that "27% of the total value of Soviet farm output comes from the private plots that occupy less than one percent of the nation's agricultural lands. At that rate, private plots are roughly 40 times as efficient as land worked collectively."[27] Although Smith later lowers this figure, he still concludes that personal plots are much more productive than kolkhoz fields. Add to this the fact that Western journalists always call the personal plot "private," and it becomes obvious that this is an argument for the fundamental superiority of private over socialized property. Yet neither the definition of the personal plot as private property, nor the notion of its miraculously high productivity stand up to scrutiny. The personal plot (a personal holding) is a small parcel of land — no larger than half a hectare. It cannot be bought, sold, leased or bequeathed. Calling it private property is unfounded and surely ideologically motivated. The kolkhoz or, rather, the state "grants" the plot to the peasant in exchange for certain clearly delineated obligations. He has the right to work the plot as long as he fulfills these obligations: his main duty being to work in the kolkhoz for a fixed number of days, usually 200-300 days a year. Otherwise he loses his plot.

Even so, personal plots remain a foreign body within the Soviet economy for two reasons. First, they are not part of the planned economy — the kolkhozniks have the right to cultivate them as they see fit. Second, the product is at the kolkhozniks' disposal and they may sell all or part of it at market prices. The personal plot cannot be studied according to the traditional categories of private or state

---

27. H. Smith, *The Russians* (New York: Quadrangle, 1975), p. 201.

property. Soviet economists, embarrassed by the unde-
fined nature of the personal plot, sometimes term it "personal property — a new, socialist-inspired economic category."[28] "A new economic category produced by Stalinism" would be theoretically more correct. Even Soviet
economists admit that when kolkoz labor went practically
unpaid "personal plots were the only incentive for labor
participation in the socialized sector."[29] The socialized
sector output was channeled by the state to the cities,
while the personal plots fed the kolkhozniks, who worked
in the kolkhoz not for wages but rather for the right to
work a personal plot or, as Timofeev says, for the
"right to live."

K.E. Wädekin correctly defines Soviet agriculture as a
symbiosis of the socialized sector and the peasant
personal plots.[30] From the first days of collectivization
onward, the socialized sector and the personal plots com-
plemented each other and — unable to exist separately —
constituted the essence of the kolkhoz system. And there
exists division of labor between the socialized and the
personal sectors. The socialized sector specializes in
highly mechanized and capital-intensive cultures (wheat,
flax, cotton), while personal plots produce non-mechanized
and labor-intensive crops (potatoes, vegetables, fruit).
This explains why a direct comparison of productivity
between the socialized and the personal sectors simply on
the basis of product volume is misleading. In Estonia, for

---

28. Cited in K.E. Wadekin, *The Private Sector in Soviet Agriculture* (Berkeley:
University of California Press, 1973), p. 11.

29. See, for example, V. Morozov, *Trudoden', den'gi i torgovlya na sele*
(Moskva: Ekonomika, 1965), p. 176.

30. K.E. Wadekin, *op. cit.*, 1973.

example, 94% of all wool is produced by personal plots, the rest in the kolkhoz. But this hardly means that labor productivity of personal plots is much higher. All it means is that, because of regional differences, Estonian collective farms produce almost no wool at all because all wool production is assigned to collective farms in other republics (where the ratio of socialized and personal wool production might be quite the opposite).

There is little doubt that personal plots contribute significantly to total agricultural production: in 1979, the plots provided 60% of the potatoes, 42% of fruit, 96% of rabbit meat, and 40% of pork and poultry produced in the country. But this still does not mean that labor productivity of personal plots is particularly high. One of the principal virtues of Timofeev's book lies in his debunking of the "private plot miracle": he simply describes, with utmost realism, how and by whom the personal plots are worked. It is no accident the book's title alludes to a phrase Kautsky dedicated to the peasant's degradation necessary for the prosperity of his small holding. But in case a dissident author should be accused of willful exaggeration, let us turn to an article of rare sincerity, published in *Voprosy Ekonomiki*, an authoritative Soviet review. G. Shmelev writes that personal plots are worked by those who cannot participate in socialized production, either for family or health reasons (women with small children, invalids) or for age reasons (children and pensioners). Also, the kolkhozniks work on their plots overtime, in addition to the long workday in the socialized sector.[31] But the labor of invalids, children, old people

---

31. G. Shmelev, "Obshchestvennoe proizvodstvo i lichnoe podsobnoe khozyaistvo," *Voprosy ekonomiki*, 1981, no. 5, p. 69.

and kolkhozniks working nights after a heavy workday cannot be particularly productive, especially as they work small parcels of land (1/8 to 1/2 hectare) by hand, using only spades and other manual tools, unable to employ machinery or to form cooperatives. The only form of mechanization known Qn the plots is the power saw (14% of the plots) and the water pump (only 3% of the plots possess such a treasure).[32] At the same time, the analysis of Soviet economists shows that whenever the crop depends above all on manual labor, the productivity of personal plots is much higher than that of the kolkhoz. According to Shmelev's data, in 1977 the fruit and berry yield of the personal plots in Bielorussia and Lithuania was 10 to 12 times higher than the kolkhoz and sovkhoz yields.[33]

All the same, these figures do not so much demonstrate the high productivity of personal plots as the incredible inefficiency of Stalin's collective farms, where the indifference of the kolkhozniks towards the result of their labor is unprecedented. Remarked the Soviet sociologist Yu. Arutinian, personal plots are more like a penalty that Soviet agriculture pays for the backwardness of its productive forces.[34]

Collective Farms in the Brezhnev Period.

Brezhnev's administrative policy towards collective farms by and large mirrored general Soviet administra-

---

32. R.V. Ryvkina, *Obraz zhizni selskogo naseleniya* (Novosibirsk: Nauka, 1979), p. 182.

33. G. Shmelev, *op. cit.*

34. Yu. Arutyunyan, *op. cit.*

tive policy of the last two decades. It was a policy of maintaining the *status quo*, a zealous conservation of the political power structure and of the administrative system created by Stalin. Terror was no longer the guiding principle of state administration, however, and the coercive apparatus was weakened and subordinated to the party-state organs. Accordingly the neo-Stalinist state relied — and continues to rely today under Chernenko — increasingly on economic stimuli, whereas compulsory labor became less frequent and lower in scale.[35] Same holds for the kolkhoz policy. On the one hand, the kolkhoz structure and management system remain basically unchanged; on the other hand, economic incentives are replacing — although gradually and inconsistently — compulsory labor. The Brezhnev period also saw a several-fold increase in state investments in agriculture. Although this did not lead to a significant rise in productivity, it did raise the kolkhozniks' standard of living. A few years ago kolkhoz residents were granted passports and consequently the right, be it only formal, to geographic mobility. State prices for agricultural products have risen considerably, although today, as even Brezhnev used to say, they often are still too low to recoup production costs.[36] In many cases the state was forced to convert collective farms into state agricultural farms — the sovkhoz, to create agrarian-industrial complexes and, finally, to transform the kolkhozniks into agricultural workers. Of course this also improved the peasants' lot.

---

35. V. Zaslavsky, *The Neo-Stalinist State. Class, Ethnicity and Consensus in Soviet Society* (Armonk, N.Y.: Sharpe, 1982).

36. *Pravda*, July 4, 1978.

Yet, by international standards, despite these recent measures, kolkhoz labor productivity remains quite low.[37] The kolkhoz system is in a state of profound and chronic crisis; massive investment may prolong its existence, but cannot cure it.

To understand why increased investment cannot much increase kolkhoz labor productivity, it is necessary to focus on the demographic-sexual structure of the kolkhoz and on the general conditions of life in the countryside. State exploitation of kolkhoz residents, together with poor material and cultural living conditions force a large number of young people, one generation after another, to flee the kolkhoz. The ablest and most enterprising succeed and, writes a Soviet author, "emigration drains the countryside of the best labor resources."[38] Consequently, between 1959 and 1975, the number of kolkhozniks declined by 30-31%, while the number of those able to work declined by 39%.[39] Since the major avenues of escape from the kolkhoz — enlistment, construction work in remote areas of the country, higher education — are mostly open to young men, the kolkhoz displays a marked disproportion between the sexes. In 1977, for example, men able to work comprised only 20.5% of the kolkhoz population. Soviet authors have often remarked on the rapid aging of the holkhoz population as well.[40]

---

37. K.E. Wadekin, *op. cit.*, 1982.

38. *Problemy istorii sovetskogo krestyanstva, op. cit.*, p. 42.

39. *Ibid.*

40. V.I. Staroverov, *Sotsial'no-demograficheskie problemy derevni* (Moskva: Nauka, 1975), p. 10.

If at this point one considers the depraved life of those who stay in the kolkhoz, the failure of massive investments to generate improved productivity becomes abundantly clear. In this connection, alcoholism is a phenomenon worth noting. One of Timofeev's great merits is his skill in depicting with stark realism the everyday life of the Soviet village. The picture Timofeev paints shows full well that unto this day the "idiocy of rural life" flourishes in the Soviet countryside. The scarcity of consumer goods, the isolation due to lacking roads and transportation, limited entertainment, the monotony and drabness of everyday life all drive the rural population to drink. Recently the Soviet press published, for the first time in many years, figures on the consumption of alcohol in the countryside: a peasant family spends 30% of its gross income on alcoholic products.[41] Even experts were surprised by this figure,[42] especially as it only indicated the consumption of state-produced alcohol and did not include the ubiquitous home-distilled vodka.

In the 1970s the crisis of the kolkhoz system intensified as a result of several consecutive years of poor harvests. Foodstuffs became increasingly scarce, and could not be replaced by foreign imports of grain, meat and other products. The situation forced the Soviet government to ration meat and dairy products in several regions. The American grain embargo demonstrated among other things that regular grain supplies room the U.S. cannot be depended on. Under the circumstances, the Brezhnev

---

41. P. Dudochkin, "Trezvost' - zakon zhizni,' *Nash sovremennik*, 1981, no. 8, p. 136.

42. Cf. *Voprosy filosofii*, 1982, no. 7, p. 113.

administration decided to take the first serious step toward restructuring the kolkhoz system: the stand of the party apparatus on the personal plots of the kolkhozniks changed radically.

The party line on personal plots was always predictably contradictory. As Timofeev writes, the plots are indispensable to the kolkhoz system insofar as they permit the state to appropriate almost all kolkhoz crops and yet not starve the peasants. On the other hand, the uncontrolled and market-oriented nature of the plots always annoyed the Soviet administration. Historically, the personal plots were subject to all possible restrictions, were called the "sores that distract people from the socialized economy, that undermine work discipline and drive people to speculation."[43] But in the late 1970s, the Soviet administration began, however, cautiously, to support personal plots; in the press personal plots were suddenly praised as "an indispensable part of the country's agrarian-industrial complex."[44] In 1981 the Central Committee promulgated "increased personal plot production" and urged the creation of a favorable social climate toward the plots.[45] The following incident helps explain how suddenly the party apparatus changed its line: in 1973, when sociologists asked a group of party leaders and agricultural specialists about "changes in the personal plots over the next 10-15 years," 12% answered that the plots "would remain the same"; 74% said "they would shrink and change character"; 12% said "they would disappear."[46]

43. *Pravda Ukrainy*, May 25, 1964.
44. G. Shmelev, *op. cit.*, p. 66.
45. *Sel'skaya zhizn'*, January 18, 1981.
46. R.V. Ryvkina, *op. cit.*, p. 186.

Not a single party leader thought the plots might grow and expand.

But like most of the reforms of the Brezhnev period, the change of policy regarding personal plots was an inconsistent half-measure. The Brezhnev administration proved incapable of embarking on the course of truly essential reform. And yet the present symbiosis of the socialized sector and the personal plots has no future whatever. Existing personal plots are unproductive and, in the words of a Siberian sociologist, are "one of the major factors that pushes young people out of the countryside."[47] Timofeev shows all too clearly the price kolkhozniks pay for the privilege of their personal plots: the second workday because of which peasants, and especially women, have literally not one moment's rest; the toil of children and old people; the self-exploitation of small producers at the price of their own health. If the agricultural crisis is to be solved by relying on personal plot production, it will be necessary to abolish obligatory kolkhoz labor or, at least, reduce the number of workdays that entitle a kolkoznik to his plot; also, to enlarge plots, introduce mechanization, allow for cooperative family labor, and so forth. But such measures would practically dismantle the kolkhoz system — something the aged Soviet leadership is absolutely not ready to do.

It is difficult to tell what direction Soviet leaders will choose to solve the agriculture problem. A likely choice appears to be the integration of collective farms into the state: that is, their conversion into state agrarian collectives like the sovkhoz, with personal plots alongside. It is

---

47. *Ibid.*, p. 185.

unlikely that Poland, where collective farms were transformed into small private holdings, would provide an inspirational model. Official writings continue to extol "the kolkhoz as a permanent form of the economy and of peasant organization,"[48] but such pronouncements are but ideological incantations. The kolkhoz — a monstrous child of Stalinism — cannot survive. Even among Soviet researchers there is a growing conviction that by 1990 the kolkhoz system and its unfortunate kolkhozniks will no longer exist.[49]

This is not to say that Timofeev's book is a realistic assessment of the Soviet leadership's economic and political choices, either in the short or in the long run. Instead it is a work that denounces the wretched living conditions of the subordinate classes in the Soviet Union, particularly of the peasants. It is also an appeal to the dissident intelligentsia to focus on the socio-economic structure and on the suffering of working people. In a sense, Timofeev reminds this intelligentsia that it is precisely an alliance with the working classes that is essential for the radical transformation of Soviet society. Clearly, Timofeev considers the system incapable of reform. He has lived through the disappointment of Khrushchev's reforms and has tried to understand the reasons behind their demise.

This has led him to conclude that the crux of the problem lies in the way the party bureaucracy, together with the technocratic strata and the scientific and humanistic intelligentsia, expropriate the socially necessary product

---

49. *Kolkhozy v ekonomicheskoi sisteme sotsializma. Sbornik statei* (Moskva: Ekonomika, 1973), p. 13.

from the working strata, particularly the peasants. This product can be extracted indefinitely, since working classes have little bargaining power[50] — and kolkhozniks none at all. There is no free market for peasant labor because the ruling strata do not find it convenient to treat labor as a commodity. As a result, labor,is easier to exploit.

Still, the ruling strata cannot dispense with the market altogether. Instead, they restrict it as much as possible for fear that a free market will reveal their uselessness and destroy the basis of their social privileges.

At this point, a word about Timofeev's use of the term "black market" is in order. In Russian, as in English, "black market" (*chernyi rynok*) implies an illegal, clandestine market — a meaning present in Timofeev's writing. For indeed, what peasants do with equipment and products stolen from the kolkhoz is black market, what workers do when they rent out the state's machinery on the side is also black market, and so is what happens with administrative appointments. For Timofeev, however, all this is but a consequence of a much greater illegality perpetrated by the state itself — and here Timofeev uses the term "black market" as a metaphor for the state's illegality, the state's crime against human nature. The Soviet state, he argues, is compelled to tolerate free market relations because without them Soviet society could not survive. This is why there is a market square for the selling of kolkhoz and personal plot products; this is why the state tolerates the worker's selling of his overtime labor on the side. But at the same time, the same Soviet state suf-

---

50. V. Zaslavsky, *op. cit.*, pp. 24-79.

focates free market relations with endless measures and prohibitions whose only purpose is to ensure the survival of the party apparatus: this, for Timofeev, is the grand illegality, the "blackness" of the market. He writes:

> For the prohibitions are the essence of power, the substance of party bureaucracy activities: the bureaucracy will do without an abundance of grain in the country. It needs no market profit; a varied and harmonious development of the economy is not essential — it needs only power, an unlimited abundance of power, profit in the form of increased power, and a system of power distribution wherein more and more power is gained as one advances in the hierarchy.

The alternative Timofeev sees is the reestablishment of a totally free market. He has unconditional faith in private initiative, reasoning that its success within the Soviet "noose of prohibitions" implies an even greater success should all the prohibitions be lifted. This credo is present in every sentence of Timofeev's book.

Timofeev unhesitatingly condemns all obstacles to movement in this direction — above all, the notion of *socialist utopia*. Socialism, he believes, prevails where there is fear of risk, the same risk that is the essence of private initiative and the wellspring of progress and well-being. According to Timofeev there is fear of risk in us all. Whenever this fear prevails, economic activity stagnates and a ruling group that identifies itself with the state and reigns over the indiscriminate exploitation of the workers usurps power.

Based on this assumption and armed with a profound, albeit polemical, knowledge of Soviet reality, Timofeev is determined to expose all attempts at reconciling socialism and the market as hypocritical and mindless. He believes such reconciliation impossible. It was attempted with the NEP (New Economic Policy), but Stalin understood what Lenin chose to ignore: if socialism and the market coexist, the latter soon prevails, for it is natural while socialism is spurious, at least in the economic sphere. Thus, in the course of his polemic, Timofeev also extols the NEP. He accuses Soviet historians of distorting history by intentionally forgetting that the period was a happy moment for Soviet peasantry. No doubt Timofeev also distorts history by forgetting the harsh reality facing the poorer peasants of the time — the *batraki* (hired laborers) and the *bedniaki* — but at least he is sure to attract the attention of all those tired of the rhetoric celebrating the triumphs of Soviet socialism.

Instead of celebrations he is after a rigorous analysis of current Soviet reality, an analysis replete with Marxist thought that ironically aims to exalt private initiative as a guarantee of better living conditions for the working classes.

At this point there should be no doubt that Timofeev sides with all the working classes (see his concluding chapter), even though his greatest sympathies lie with the peasantry. He does indeed refer to the opposition between the city and the country, drawing on the populist tradition which survived in the Russian culture even after the October revolution. Timofeev's populism, however, contains no mystical preference for the countryside, no glorification of the peasants and their morality. Perhaps

Timofeev's attitude toward the peasants is similar to Czeslaw Milosz's feelings for the Lithuanian peasants of his youth, when Lithuania was still independent: they were no better than others, so why should they suffer more?[51]

And thus Timofeev's book will remain one of the most important documents on the Soviet kolkhoz system and kolkhoz life which he describes with sympathy and realism. Future historians will remember this work, long after the official texts extolling the fictional achievements of the kolkhoz system are forgotten. It clearly exposes the Stalinist heritage of the Soviet Union today; it continues the best traditions of Russian democratic intelligentsia and stands as one of the finest achievements of Soviet dissent of the late 1970s.

Unfortunately, in addition to exhibiting the powerful critical thought of the Soviet opposition, Timofeev's book also demonstrates how far this opposition is from offering a realistic political program for transforming society. To Western readers Timofeev's hope that a free market could replace the black market in the Soviet Union or that, if allowed to operate without state restrictions, the market economy would pave the way toward social democratization may sound like a bad joke, neo-liberalism notwithstanding. Z. Bauman, who has lived and studied in both East and West, observes that:

> Society cannot rely on the market for the provision of the basic conditions of its existence. Rather, it has to defend itself against the disasters which the chaotic reality

---

51. C. Milosz, *The Captive Mind* (New York: Random House, 1961).

of the market can inflict. Such basic conditions can be still provided; not, however,
without an active and positive economic
programme adopted and consistently pur-
sued by the (traditionally seen as non-
economic) powers of the state. Contrary to
the old optimism . . . the market cannot
guarantee the balancing of the total output
with the total demand; unemployment is,
therefore, its organic and ineradicable
proclivity.[52]

However, it is unfair in this case to criticize Timofeev
for glossing over the experience of economic development in other industrialized countries. It is not just a
question of human solidarity, but of considering the
actual conditions in which a Soviet intellectual operates.
Like several generations of Soviet intellectuals before
him, Timofeev is completely cut off from Western experience. What he knows of the West is probably as little
as a Western reader knows of the life of the Soviet kolkhoz.
Timofeev's book is, unwittingly, a document on the pre-
vailing spiritual climate among Soviet intellectuals. Decades of boundless exploitation have led Soviet peasants to
extreme alienation from socialized labor. State-run exploitation of the kolkhoz has dealt such a blow to the idea
of collective labor and socialized property that even the
words kolkhoz (short for *kollektivnoe khoziaistvo* — collective economy, collective estate) and kolkhoznik have acquired in Russian a pejorative connotation associated
with the basest form of social life.

---

52. Z. Bauman, *Memories of Class. The Pre-history and Afer-life of Class* (London: Routledge and Kegan Paul, 1982), p. 164.

That the idea of collective labor, the idea of freely associated producers and their democratic self-management could have lost all appeal in Soviet society (as Timofeev demonstrates), should hardly come as a surprise. And this is yet another crime of Stalinism.

Chapter I

I am not a peasant. And I have never starved. It was only accidentally that I happened to observe the life of a peasant family at close quarters, and it was only when I began (rather casually) to note down the circumstances and events of that life that I suddenly realized with amazement that the entire Soviet system — from our high and mighty government to our learned atom-mongers and golden throated bards — leeches on the rural peasant household.

Had I shown such amazement in the twenties, I would have been blind. At that time everyone knew that the proletarian state could not survive without robbing the peasant; it was all but announced on the front page. Some accepted this enthusiastically, while others were loathe to accept it at all, but everyone knew. This knowledge faded somewhat with time and talk about the people's state, but the system's dependence on the peasant remains — only our conception of it has changed. Whereas in the twenties people knew what was happening in the countryside, now, fifty years later, we have the well-rehearsed myth of the flourishing collective farmer, which in no way accords with the economic facts. Nor are we, the gullible children of socialism, any too keen on bringing our ideas in line with reality.

We city dwellers do not know the countryside or the

laws by which the peasant lives; knowledge of rural life has been replaced by lies and preconceptions passed on from generation to generation. It rarely happens that a hereditary city dweller — or even a recent one — becomes ashamed of his smug ignorance and disregard for the peasant's labor and welfare. Time has the effect of blinding us still more to our own ignorance and indifference, rather than opening our eyes. "At least nowadays the peasant has enough," assert our intellectuals; those who some ten or fifteen years ago mulled over the rural theme, who were preoccupied with the destiny of the Russian village, and who, to this day, subscribe to *Novyy mir*. "A time of plenty has now arrived for the peasant," they say, evidently relying on newspaper accounts.

But why focus only on today? We have always thought of the peasant as having plenty. I remember a strange anecdote from my childhood, bitingly told by someone in my city-dwelling family. A peasant, so the story goes, brought a bag of money to exchange at the time of the first post-war currency reform. The money was counted, and found to be one ruble short of a hundred thousand. "Damn it," complained the peasant, "I brought the wrong bag. The other one has a hundred thousand even." Where would a peasant get a bag of money in a time of famine? This is a perplexing story, with its typically Stalinist approach to the peasant: squeeze him dry and he will come up with more. Or no: the anecdote expresses not so much perplexity as hope — if the peasant has bags of money, then all is well with the country. There is nothing to worry about, the country will survive; that is, there is *something left to take* and *someone left to take it from*. As long as a man is alive, something can be taken from him. The question of whether to take from the peasant does not exist for our government. Take as much as possible, take everything! But how? Thus is a question all right, which leads to a whole set of questions.

How is it possible that the expensive space program, the grandoise but ineffectual economic undertakings in our country, and even successful military operations in Ethiopia, are all financed out of the peasant family's modest budget? Is it the peasant family alone that pays for party and government policy? What is the general mechanism for the exploitation of the working man under developed socialism? The peasant question falls entirely within this range. Marxist political analysis is of no use here. Classical laws of capitalist production and the free market do not apply — neither exists. But it is possible to do without the market entirely only within the theoretical constructs of Soviet political economists; human needs are so vast and various that they cannot be confined to any norms, regulations or plans imposed from above. We look for an economic response to our very existence, outside of plans and regulations. And we find it.

The longer the relatively peaceful period lasts without war, revolution or mass repression the more the Soviet socio-economic system takes on the appearance of a colossal black market. This black market exists and develops openly, right before everyone's eyes. Within its framework, it is possible to feed the country with potatoes or to build a diesel locomotive, to enroll one's son in the university or to buy an agronomist diploma, to repair a tractor or obtain a plot in Moscow's "exclusive" cemetery. Everything is bought and sold outside plans and regulations. One hand washes the other. But who comes out ahead? Nobody does, and we'll never get free from our poverty.

Sometimes the black market — that art of breathing within the noose of prohibitions and restrictions, that simple-minded slyness, that subterfuge of paupers — seems to be designed to deceive the Soviet government. Force us into collective farms and we'll till our individual household plots; impose shortages and rationing and we'll bribe and get ours on the side; feed us lean cafeteria food and we'll raise rabbits in our apartments; offer us a lousy doctor at the end of a long queue and we'll troop to a good one with a gift. But do we end up on top? Not on your life!

If necessary, the authorities will stifle personal plot production with restrictions and levies (nothing new, to say the least); the police will rid the apartment of rabbits and even a doctor will catch a jail term for receiving his gifts. Our disingenuous trickery could not survive otherwise. We are on a leash just loose enough to breathe, nothing more.

The black market is not just the loophole, the secret doorway we cut in the wall, it is both the loophole and the wall itself. At first sight, the black market appears to lead a marginal existence and to play a subordinate role in the planned economy. But closer examination shows that the black market is the very basis of the Soviet economy, the foundation on which the planned economic structure rests. The black market is the socialist mechanism of power and exploitation, the very essence of our socio-economic system, more obviously so in recent times.

The commodities which circulate in the black market

support the existing political and social order. How, exactly, do they do this? In what direction is society heading? To understand this, we must first understand the black market itself and its technology. This technology is the real political economy of socialism. Under existing political conditions, we know no other. Is there an alternative? The sixty-year history of the Soviet state attests to the fact that restriction of private initiative leads to speculation, corruption, and secret exploitation. It is difficult to imagine any other outcome, no matter where the Soviet experiment might be implemented.

But we are not quite ready to understand. Soviet society, in its essence, is a socialist economic system absolutely unique in history (despite any analogies which may have occurred to scholars), and its analysis demands entirely new methods and concepts. These do not yet exist. Therefore we must proceed more descriptively than analytically, not so much with the scientific method as with graphic impressions, personal experience, and individual examples. As a journalist, I may find it easier to undertake this mixture of reporting and scholarship than would a serious scholar.

Where shall we begin? Where *can* we begin? There is only one sector of the black market, the discussion of which has only recently — under the threat of general famine — been permitted and even encouraged: the **peasant's personal plot. This happens to be our chief** interest! The peasant's yard shall be our starting point.

Chapter II

I arrived at the village on March 27 of last year in a blinding snowstorm. It was on that day that Aksinya Egoryevna Khovracheva was buried, but I was not present. I actually saw the burial taking place, but I did not go. I did not understand what was going on, and didn't ask who had died. Her coffin passed right by me, I saw the pine boards out of the corner of my eye, but in the dense, driving snow I couldn't make out what those boards were or who was carrying them. I was hurrying home, out of the blizzard and into the warmth. It crossed my mind that some carpenters were getting together. A lot of building and remodeling had been going on. I couldn't see the mourners at all, because of the snow. Or else I saw the mourners but not the coffin: big crowd, could be some kind of wedding, or maybe they just got some herring in at the store . . . The snowstorm banished all concern for others. It was only in the evening that they came and told me what sort of house they'd been building and what sort of wedding they were celebrating.

I first became acquainted with Aksinya Egoryevna Khovracheva and her husband Aleksandr Avdeich (nicknamed The Drunky) many years ago when I bought a house near theirs and went to spend several months there fishing, mushrooming, and writing a dissertation on the melodics of Russian verse. We met for the first time one rainy autumn afternoon, which I shall always remember as a dark, incomprehensible nightmare, but which for Aksinya Egoryevna may not have been all that unusual. The Drunky got drunk, beat her senseless, then dragged her by the hair out into the yard and with his free hand began fumbling around: he was looking for an axe to behead her, as their four daughters looked on, paralyzed with fear.

Would he have killed her? Surely not The Drunky, not that frail, pathetic little *muzhik*. Murder never crossed his mind, he was just fooling around. But who knows what a drunken man will do? Aksinya Egoryevna herself used to tell about the night —a year before I first came to Gati — when a drunken man was fooling around and killed three of his children by assiduously setting fire to the four corners of the house. They rescued his wife and would not let her back into the burning house. As if that weren't enough, she confessed that it was all her fault: God was punishing her for her abortions. She'd had the abortions because her last child by the drunkard had been born completely simple — he'd been sent to a hospital at the age of two. He was the ony child to survive. "How many simple ones would she have to bear for those three to live?" asked Aksinya Egoryevna. This was the only time I heard her really complain.

Aksinya Egoryevna and I were next-door neighbors for many years. I witnessed her infrequent moments of happiness, such as the wedding of her third daughter, the deaf Raya, to a fine and modest lad, policeman in Ryazan. I watched Akasinya Egoryevna walk proudly through the village showing her friends and relatives the diploma received by her youngest daughter, Anna, who was trained as a dental technician. I saw her decline to drive down the village street in the new *Moskvich* when her son paid his one and only visit. He worked as a fitter on a construction site in Egypt or somewhere else in Africa. She was embarrassed for some reason to get into the car, but she stood and accepted the congratulations of neighbors and passers-by as the car drove up and down the village.

I heard her grieving and lamenting when her Aleksandr Avdeich died. Though her daughters were supporting her, she fainted from grief in their arms at the cemetery. The daughters were restrained in their weeping. Had they loved the deceased as their mother had, or pitied him as much?

Yes, Aksinya Egoryevna was lavish in her joy and grief, resigned to injury and suffering, but the quality that struck me most was her great, multifaceted talent for managing, and her boundless capacity for work. When electricity came to Gati twenty years ago, one of the grown daughters sent her a meter. The meter was installed, and it turned out that Aksinya Egoryevna had used eight kopecks' worth of electricity during the entire summer. She got up the crack of dawn and went to bed when it was scarcely dark. She was too tired from excessive labor to sit idle in the evenings, and all the work was outdoors — on the collective farm, her own personal plot, or in the forest clearing and haymaking. I don't know about winter, but from May through October, Aksinya Egoryevna had need of a light in the evenings only to find her bed in the darkness and to pour the cat's milk into the saucer without spilling it.

Watching the Khovrachevs' efforts year after year, I

came to respect increasingly the skill with which the peasant family avoided destitution, making do with only a tiny plot of land. It was nearly impossible to keep livestock for lack of fodder, and there had been no opportunity to earn on the side — on the collective farm or anywhere else — for decades. Yet the Khovrachevs remained a peasant family: a family that feeds itself and the whole nation by its own labor on its own land. Aksinya Egoryevna was the head of that family. She ran the whole enterprise for twenty years without a husband and became accustomed to relying only on herself. Even when he was still alive he hadn't been good for much, since he started drinking as a young man and grew sickly as he got older. So it was all of forty-five years, not twenty, that she had fed and clothed them all and give them a start in life. The children all grew up, studied, and established themselves. Aksinya Egoryevna fed them all, not from some magical income and certainly not with collective farm earnings, which she never saw, but from her own tiny orchard. An acre — from a bird-cherry tree to an apple tree and eighty paces deep — was all the authorities left the family after collectivization. Here she worked and put her children to work. This was her field, her hope, and there was nothing but herself and this land on which to depend. What would she have done without her orchard with eight mouths to feed? Nothing. Without this garden it would have been impossible to survive. As long as she has her own land and huse, she makes her own fortune — as she sows, so shall she reap. Of course, technically the land does not belong to her, but to the collective farm or even to the state. It has to be earned by working on the collective farm, but there, too, Aksinya Khovracheva is always on the Honor Board: she has always been a hard worker.

The tales of her work on the collective farm were almost legendary. And I myself remember very well the days, fifteen years ago, when she still went out to work. She was already past sixty at the time. The foreman would stop every morning in front of her house and without getting out of his cart, call out, "Oksya! Come out to pick!" It sounded as if he was calling Aksinya Egoryevna to some small job — something somewhere had to be picked, perhaps a few flowers and then she could come back. Actually, it was a matter of weeding, one of the hardest, most tedious kinds of fieldwork: bent double in the hot sun, always on your feet and moving, without an end in sight, because it is impossible to weed all the *kolkhoz* fields by hand — by the time you reach the far end the near one is all overgrown again.

In the evening the reason for this industriousness on *kolkhoz* land would become perfectly clear: Aksinya Egoryeva would return with a garland of waste grass. Apart from the extra work-days, which they would be paid for God knows when and how ("Will they even be paid for this year?"), this grass was the chief prize. Weeders were permitted to help themselves. The coarse hay would do for feeding the stock, and I think that this was sufficient incentive, for there was always a problem with hay.

Money was of little importance in the collective farmer's income; only in the last ten years has he been paid even a little money for the working day. Payment in kind was also of secondary importance, although the three or four bags of rye which might be the payment for a year's backbreaking work meant a lot to the peasant family. The main thing was the right to buy straw and hay for one's own cattle, the right to mow hay, and, finally and most importantly, the right to a personal plot, to half a hectare of land, the right to run a private farm. Sometimes the peasants worked on the collective farm for no pay at all, for neither money or payment in kind, but in return they enjoyed their right to a personal plot, for otherwise it would have been impossible to realize that other right not granted by governments — the *right to life.*

Stalin said in 1935 that "if the collective does not have an abundance of produce and cannot give the individual collective-farm workers and their families everything they need, then the collective farm cannot undertake to satisfy both public and private needs."[1] In those years peasants comprised three-fourths of the population of the country, but the peasant family was, as it were, outside society. Its needs did not deserve attention. "The collective farm cannot undertake...." Nor did the government concern itself unduly with the well-being of peasants and their families. "In 1939 about 16,000 collective farms did not pay for work with money; 46,000 collective farms paid only two kopecks per work-day; about 9,000 collective farms did not pay any grain per work day."[2] These official statistics cover as many as a third of all the collective farms in the land, six million peasant families. How many hungry mouths do these statistics represent? We do not know, just as we know little about the life of peasants on those collective farms which paid an average of three or four kopecks and a half-kilo of grain per work day.

---

1. *Second All-Union Congress of Kolkhoz Shock-workers,* stenographic transcript (1935), p. 1.

2. G.V. Dyachkov, *Obshchestvennoe i lichnoe v kolkhozakh* (Moscow, 1968), p. 22.

Perhaps not so many people starved in the years just before the war, fewer than in the fatal year of 1933, for they were beginning to learn to feed themselves by relying only on the personal plots. But the government was also learning to squeeze the peasants ever more tightly, ever more relentlessly, and to take away their personal property for the benefit of "society." In 1939, after the regular plenum of the Central Committee of the party, more than 2.5 million hectares of personal land were taken away from the peasants; "surplus" land was diverting attention from the official economy and allowing the peasants to preserve some slight degree of independence.

The authorities generally considered the prosperity, even the sheer survival of the farm family, to be completely incidental or perhaps even a harmful excess. Not only was the farmer denied everything produced on the collective farm by his labor, but the private parcel, the personal farming to feed his family, was heavily taxed. Each farm yard, regardless of the family composition, delivered the mandatory quotas of milk, meat, eggs, wool, and hides. In addition, there was a monetary tax — some paid a hundred rubles, some even more. This monetary tax was an astonishing invention of the Soviet treasury: a tax on products already surrendered to government, a tax on a tax.

The terms were harsh: "after the tax deadline the people's court is to consider the inventory of the defaulter's property and effect the removal of the property in such quantity as to repay the debt."[3] But where is

---

3. "Zakon o sel'skokhozyastvennom naloge," Sept. 1, 1939, p. 34b.

money to be had, if the collective farm pays its workers nothing? Why, the very same personal plots, of course: the peasant would simply sell his produce; even if hungry himself.

But hopeless as the life of Aksinya Egoryevna and her fellow villagers was in the first decade after collectivization, impoverished as the Russian peasantry was by 1941 (and the peasant of central Russia, where the soil is poor, always had it especially hard); senseless as work on the land had become, the war added yet further sufferings, which finally laid waste to the peasantry. The first fifteen post-war years alternated between hunger and famine. But extortion from the peasant's plot went on all those years, as milk, meat, and eggs passed before the eyes of hungry children. Society cannot concern itself with the suffering of peasant children.

The crippling levies were officially repealed in 1958, but the local authorities were immediately saddled with quotas for the aforesaid products. Since for local officials good standing was directly dependent on the fulfillment of the quotas, they literally forced the peasants to deliver to the state, for a minuscule restitution, the same products levied prior to 1958. And the peasants delivered — what choice did they have? One needs a passport to leave the collective farm, a passport which the authorities will never issue; and without one, one cannot obtain work or lodging. The peasant was chained to his collective farm.

Aksinya Egoryevna remembered well the unpaid labor, the monetary tax, and the tax in produce. She remembered how the right to a personal farm — the right to life — was purchased. She remembered, and though she tried to talk about it, she could not, because she would always start to cry. There were six little ones at home, after all. It is horrible to think about hungry children after twenty years, or even thirty, even though, thank God, none of them died.

Aksinya Egoryevna does not have to confirm her rights any longer; she now receives a pension of twenty-five rubles from the government and ten rubles from the collective farm. It is true that this is similar to the life pension of an invalid, less than the lowest pension of a city-dweller, but on the other hand, the rural pensioner gets to keep his plot as long as he lives in the village. If you can cope with a garden in your old age, the entire market profit is yours. What else could a lone old woman want?

Aksinya Egoryevna's youngest daughter wanted her to move to town. She urged her mother to procure a passport, leave the farm and come live with her, since the husband had been promised an apartment in the near future. The mother's arrival and possible death shortly thereafter (she wasn't exactly young, after all) promised some extra square feet of living space. But, despite the fact that Aksinya Egoryevna had gotten used to being in town over the last few years, and despite her pity for her daughter, the idea of giving up her acre of land — where year after year she had planted and then sold potatoes, and also smaller amounts of cucumbers, tomatoes and other staple vegetables — was absolutely out of the question. She would feel like an orphan.

I was not surprised, therefore, when during one of my stays in the village, Aksinya Egoryevna came to see me carrying a blank sheet of paper, an envelope, and another scrap of paper with her daughter's address written on it.

"Write them that I won't be coming in the summer," she said, "and not to be offended. Say the land won't let me go. How can I leave my potatoes? They say the state store will take them for ten kopecks a kilo. And they themselves will be needing potatoes, there in town, I shouldn't wonder if they're getting more expensive to buy . . ."

She sat in silence as I wrote the letter and then read it aloud, but as she took the sealed envelope, suddenly out of the blue she said: "who saddled us with such misery?" She asked simply, as if I could and had to answer just as simply and briefly. But no, she did not expect an answer. And it was not a question, just a human being sighing from weariness.

Chapter III

Just twenty kilometers as the crow flies from Gati (Aksinya Egoryevna's village) lies the village of Posady. But while Gati is obviously a poor village of slate-roofed and even thatched wooden houses, Posady does not have a single wooden house. All the houses are of masonry, and spacious by village standards: two or three rooms, large windows, enormous terraces, and the obligatory galvanized roof. In spring all this luxury magically disappears behind a pinkish-white cloud of blossoming trees, while in autumn it is the other way round: the white stone walls and mirror-like roofs can be seen from a great distance on the rain-blackened shore. Whence the wealth in such a poor place?

There is no magic or mystery about it. All the income of Posady comes from individual plots. Here they plant no potatoes, onions, or cabbage, but only early cucumbers. The crop ripens in June and is transported by car to markets in Moscow, Ryazan, Penza, and even beyond, thanks to the nearby highway. In the fall, apples are shipped to the same markets.

Peasants with even the tiniest plots will always try to raise a cash crop rather than run an all-around farm, because the family's needs are greater than the basic foodstuffs that can be grown on a farm. In a good year, a plot at Posady will bring in up to five thousand rubles. The people of Posady take that money and buy potatoes, onions, and whatever else they need in nearby villages. Five thousand is not all that much for a family of four or five, but it is enough to have a bit left over after buying food. Nowadays the collective farm even pays a little: a good machine-operator might get 1,500 or 2,000 rubles a year.

Every time she travelled past Posady on the way home from visiting her daughter in town, our friend Aksinya Egoryevna was so struck by the difference in income that she magnified the discrepancy to unreal proportions. "Look how some people live! Once I stopped at one of their houses for drink of water, and you should see what they've got! You could even see it through the door. Just think, they put the television in the hall, as if it's nothing to them. 'We watch that one when the big one's out of order,' she says. And shows me the big one in the main room. Where does the money come from? We work just as hard and look at our wooden house — like living in a kennel."

"I know that house," I objected. "That man earns money on the side by repairing television sets. Could that have been someone's broken set out in the hall?"

Aksinya Egoryevna fell silent. She disliked arguments, but it was obvious that she kept to her own opinion about the wealth of Posady peasants as measured in television sets.

Another time she caught sight of a roadside field planted with nothing but cabbages, and this astounded her. "Why so much? Or are they some kind of foreigners who eat nothing but cabbage?"

"Perhaps it's for the market?"

"But why? Cabbage goes for 30 kopecks a head. Let's say 2,000 heads — that only makes 600 rubles. Why, we made that much from potatoes some years, with enough left over the feed ourselves and the animals all winter. That's potatoes! But cabbage is a lot of trouble. You have to water it in the spring, pick worms in summer . . . No, it's not worth it."

I was always impressed by the accuracy of Aksinya Egoryevna's calculations when it came to her everyday affairs, though she was illiterate, and needless to say, had never been trusted with anything but manual work on the collective farm.

"Wait a minute! Maybe they sell sauerkraut?" This new idea turned her thoughts in a completely different direction. "Why of course, sauerkraut! You can get fifty to eighty kopecks for sauerkraut at the market! And when a holiday's coming up — a hundred. Also it's heavier, sauerkraut. It has salt in it, and salt collects moisture. So that's what they're selling! That's where the money is! You could make thousands. And what's there to pickling cabbage? Any old woman could manage . . ."

All these discoveries excited her very much, and I thought for a while that in her old age my neighbor might go into the sauerkraut business so she could afford to buy a large television set.

I had long been familiar with her constant willingness to put into circulation her only ready capital, her own two hands. This had more than once enabled her to sell her potatoes for a good price or to get some free skim milk from the dairy for the animals' mash or even to make herself some cheese. Now, once more, she seemed to be on the verge of taking action. Something of the sort must have crossed her mind, for the next day she was rather sad.

"We were talking about cabbage," she reminded me. "Well, cabbage won't work for us. First, because we're too far from the highway. Cabbage is good to sell in winter, but our roads are impossible when it snows. Even if you could hire a driver, it would eat up all the profits. And it's not a good idea, even apart from the road. You'd have to have your own machine, you couldn't shred it by hand. You'd need barrels. At least nine barrels, it isn't worth it otherwise. Then you'd need a big cellar for the barrels . . . And besides, it takes experience. Otherwise you couldn't grow that much cabbage. The worms would get it, something would go wrong. Those people must have been growing cabbage for quite a while, they know the ropes."

Some know the ropes, others do not. Not so naive an explanation as it might seem. Custom, or in other words, tradition and experience in the form of continued application of the peasant's small capital of labor and knowledge to his personal plot, has as a special significance: the villager will not take needless risks by introducing innovations into his private farming. The harvest from his own land is too valuable to him. I am sure that Aksinya Egoryevna was not the only one who thinght about going to market with sauerkraut or some other goods more profitable than the traditional potatoes. But given the indefatigable control of the government, which has more than once tightened its screws on individual farming, one needs a specially favorable combination of circumstance and faith to risk introducing innovations. The peasant may be tenacious once the business is underway, but he is cautious.

This peasant life — seemingly peripheral to the collective farm, but essential to the collective farmer — demands a significantly more responsible business approach than does the required work on the collective farm. There, no matter what the powers-that-be may command, whatever stupidity they may let loose, it is carried out immediately — whether good or bad for the harvest — without anyone batting an eyelash. But here, all the initiative, capital, means of production, and the entire final product belong to the peasant. Here he is master. Here he is a *man*. Here he is a sort of microcosm of the farmer he could have become if his cattle and land had not been taken from him in 1930, leaving him with only a trifling plot.

The peasants can eke out a living, however scanty, as long as they can realize a part of their working time — a part of their strength — outside the economic system; not in the regular, regimented socialist system, but in the marketplace. The peasant market, restricted to the confines of the market square, is distorted by the feudal personal dependence of the collective farmer on the administrative authority. It generally has the appearance of an appendage to that main "bazaar" where they trade in party positions and demagogic values, such as the promise of the general welfare of the people and the imminent victory of communism. Yet it is a real market, and a market which the socialist government cannot do without.

Even on the surface, the statistics are shocking: personal parcels are variously estimated to make up from 1.5 to 2.5 percent of all the cultivated land in the country, and peasant farming has at its disposal only a tenth of all productive funds in agriculture. Still, peasant farms produces a third of all agricultural products — and this according to official figures![4]

But official figures ignore the fact that no less than a third of the agricultural production on the collective and state farms is lost: in the field, in transport, in storage, in the first processing. For example, according to some statistics, up to half of the potato crop is lost. By calculating the gross product in terms of price, official statistics also gloss over the fact that the government purchasing prices for grains — produced mainly by the collective and state farms — are significantly inflated, while prices for meat, vegetables, potatoes (in other words, products which are most widespread on the peasant farms) are deflated.

Official statistics are misleading, for otherwise it would be necessary to admit that in aggregate volume of the *consumed* agricultural production the share of the peasants' personal parcels, with their 2.5 percent of tilled land, is much more than half. And more: in the Baltic republics, the share of individual farming in the aggregate agricultural product — even according to official data — makes up almost half (43.6 percent in Lithuania, for example). At the same time, "50.5 percent of total earnings of the families of collective farmers in the Republic of Lithuania in 1971 were obtained from individual farming."[5]

---

4. G.I. Shmelev, *Lichnoe podsobnoe khozyaystvo i ego svyazi s obshchestvennym proizvodstvom* (Moscow, 1971), p. 11.

5. L.-I.S. Vilimavichus, *Lichnoe podsobnoe khozyaystvo pri sotsializme, ego mesto, rol' i tendentsiya razvitiya*, Dissertation abstract (1976), pp. 3, 19.

These figures are a disgrace of the Soviet economic system and a bane for the peasants whose initiative and talent are constrained by the small size of their personal orchard's and the enormous number of administrative prohibitions. It is the peasants' bane, but also their hope. Food production within the peasant economy feeds all rural inhabitants — 40 percent of the population. Moreover, even according to official statistics, it produces half of all the marketed potatoes, not less than a third of the eggs, and a third of the marketed meat — products sold to feed a significant proportion of the urban population. Without the peasant farms the socialist economy would not survive a day.

It has proved impossible to regulate the economy in its entirety. The economy is a mechanism where a planned bureaucratic system will creak and grind to a halt without a link to the flywheel of market relations worked out by the entire history of mankind. The market is the basis of the economy. Destroy it, and you destroy the national economy. This was well understood by Stalin when he **drove the peasants out onto personal plots: "the collective farm cannot undertake . . ." As long as market relations** are viable, a socialist economy can be added on, even if these are *black-market* relations subject to government administration. The black market is precisely what the authorities need. But this will be discussed later. For the time being, let us see how the peasant's minute orchard feeds the country.

How is it that Posady grows rich on early vegetables? In the first place, the village is well situated; it used to be linked to the city market by a river, and now also by a highway from farm to counter, with no time wasted.

Second, because the soil here is rich — an island of black earth in a sea of sandy loam and *podzol* — the harvest is bigger, and vegetables ripen sooner and need less watering. Who can compete? Posady has the best soil of all the well-situated villages.

At the market everyone sells at the same price, which is adjusted to poor soil conditions. Who would grow vegetables otherwise, without profit? Thus Posady makes the most of all the cucumber growers, since their cucumbers are the cheapest to grow and sell for the same price as the rest. They pocket the difference. This is textbook political economy; to some extent, the black market passes for a traditional open market, thus enticing the peasant.

Although they may not be familiar with textbook economics, the peasants long ago caught onto market mechanisms and put them into practice. This has occurred not only in central Russia or, say, Moldavia — where recently "collective farms have cut down on the sowing of grain, a less intensive crop, and increased cultivation of grapes and fruit — more intensive and profitable crops,"[6] but most of all in Georgia, the autonomous republics of the Northern Caucasus, the Baltic republics, and Belorussia, where individual plot yields more than half the peasant family's aggregate income.[7] "Potatoes from Kursk travel to Donbass markets; fruit from Central Asia and Transcaucasia goes to the city markets of central Russia; Ukrainian onions to Moscow, Gorky, Tula and so on. The Ryazan and Lipetsk regions play an especially important role in supplying Moscow markets with products from personal plots."[7]

---

6. V.I. Shubkin, *Sotsiologicheskie opyty* (Moscow, 1970), p. 78.

7. Shmelev, *op. cit.*, p. 11.

The possibility of using one's own labor to maximum advantage, moves people to truly great agricultural feats. Take, for example, the strawberry growing around large cities, where the yields (and consequently the profits) from a few hundredths or even thousandths of a hectare are beyond the wildest dreams even of our Aksinya Egoryevna, for all her lively imagination.

The writer V. Soloukhin describes this burgeoning trend:

> To wind up our botanical tour, they took me to a place called the hothouse . . .
> "Fourteen square meters," explained the proprietor. "An artificial climate. A crop whenever you like, at any time of year. But I aim for the first of the year." "Cucumbers or tomatoes? Fresh cucumber for New Year's dinner is, of course, priceless. The same goes for tomatoes." "What are you talking about! Cucumbers are coarse and cheap."
> "Then what New Year's crop are you talking about?" "Flowers. Tulips. That's what. Two or three rubles a flower. These fourteen meters bring in five thousand rubles."[8]

Is two rubles a lot or a little? What about a ruble or a ruble-and-a-half for a kilo of potatoes in Central Asia? A ruble or two for a lemon in Novosibirsk? This is expensive, very expensive! But such is the *market* price, and no one is so altruistic as to charge a dime for lemons. When it comes to market relations, a kind heart and fine morals

---

8. V. Soloukhin, "Trava," in *Nauka i zhizn'*, no. 10, 1978.

are of no use. The market has its own laws that are objective in nature. Therefore it is naive to criticize audacious Caucasians for selling peaches or oranges at high prices. The market seller has no soul. He is strictly an economic figure, with the whole Soviet system behind him.

The narrow-minded view that peasants from the Caucasus and Central Asia make exorbitant profits at central Russian markets is false. When market takings are divided among all the member sof the peasant family, it turns out, for example, that "in 1966 Turkmenistan had the highest family income of any Soviet republic, and the ninth highest per capita. At the same time, Estonia was first per capita and seventh per household."[9]

No, peasant greed is not the cause of high market prices. Those glorious five thousand, which figure from time to time as the maximum income from individual farming, represent the income of a family of at least four or five people. This is not pure profit, but only market receipts, farming expenditures can be quite high. High market prices are hardly making the peasant the richest man in the land. The actual monetary income of a peasant family is no higher, and in the vast majority of cases lower, than the average income of the worker's family with two wage earners (294 rubles per month, according to official data).

No, it is not the peasant who drives market prices up. Tulips, early cucumbers, the first tomatoes in May, and the meat at any time are expensive only because they are produced in small quantities on a small scale. The peasant cannot expand production. The size of his farm is

---

9. Shmelev, *op. cit.*, p. 26.

limited administratively, and no private cooperation is permitted. Large agricultural enterprises (collective and state farms) are designed not to satisfy direct consumer demand, but to carry out the government's trade and distribution policies for the convenience of the party bureaucracy — the ruling structure that protects the *status quo* and thereby itself. The policies of this ruling structure determine prices and levels of capital investment — direct and indirect — and ultimately determine the volume of production. The distant glimmer of consumer demand barely penetrates the darkness of bureaucratic relations. But why speak of tulips when for decades agriculture has been so meagerly financed and provided for, so poorly organized, that we cannot get bread, meat, or milk from the big farms in sufficient quantities.

Myopic discussions of blatant price-gauging should therefore be postponed at least until an explanation is found for the high prices and the shortage of food in the country. Then it will become clear whose conscience is involved. Generally speaking, nothing good results when the soul (in the mystical sense of the word) gets involved in market relations. I know of a collective farm in Central Asia whose personal plots are more fertile than any around, but whose peasants are worse off than their neighbors. The reason is that their land is washed by the waters of a sacred spring and, according to Muslim law, it is forbidden — taboo — to sell anything that grows there. The taboo makes it unnecessary to look for the most marketable varieties of apples and grapes, or to dig trenches for citrus crops. What was good enough for their forefathers is good enough for them. Ideological inhibitions have smothered economic possibilities and hindered initiative.

Can it be then that *ideological inhibitions* are impeding the growth of the whole national economy? Private initiative is taboo! Market relations are taboo! Striving for gain is taboo! Never mind that we import grain across one ocean (from America) and meat across another (from New Zealand). Our economy is thoroughly washed with the sacred ideas of Marx-Engels-Lenin (I was about to add Stalin, but that's not done today, although really, why not?).

It could be suggested that the existing prohibitions are a dismal error, a temporary misunderstanding that will disappear as the gap between the population's need for food and the low productivity of peasant labor. But there is a scant possibility of socialist agriculture's satisfying that need. Let us not delude ourselves. The prohibitions are far from accidental. They are an instrument of the *ruling structure*, an instrument of the party bureaucracy, a means of preserving the existing order. All the prohibitions are designed to protect the government of the party officials from assault by an economically strengthened peasantry or a politically-aware technostructure.

Stalin understood this best. Although the present party leadership pretends to spurn his legacy, it was Stalin, of all the exponents of Marxism, who came closest to the policy of the current ruling class. "Is the central goal of the Five-Year Plan an increase in labor productivity in the Soviet Union?" he asked in his famous speech against Bukharin. "No, it is not. For we do not need any and every kind of increase in labor productivity. We need a particular growth of labor productivity, namely, that which contributes to the dominance of the socialist sector of the national economy [that is, the non-market sector directly controlled by the party bureaucracy and objectively working to strengthen its power — L.T.] over the capitalist sector."[10]

The prohibitions are the essence of power, the substantive activity of the party bureaucracy. It can do without an abundance of grain in the country; it needs no market profit; a diversified, well-balanced economy is not essential. It needs only power, an unlimited abundance of power, profit in the form of increased power, and a system of power distribution wherein more and more power is gained as one advances in the hierarchy.

Since the party bureaucracy (like the degenerating class of feudal landlords of yore) in no way participates in the production of material and spiritual values, in what we term progress, it can avoid being swept away by that current only by imposing a strict system of prohibitions, restrictions and "taboos." All the "measures effected by the party and the government in the area of economics" which are proclaimed each time as a great gift to the people, are nothing but the efforts of a timid navigator to avoid self-imposed dams and barriers, maneuvers to keep the ship afloat. On the other hand, the *black market* poses no threat to the stability of the present government. On the contrary, it is totally under the government's control — and therefore to its advantage. Indeed, the collective farm system was conceived as a black market system from the very beginning, and its scope is considerably broader than the market square. Back to Stalin: "And if you do not have an abundance of products on your collective farm and are unable to give the collective farmers and their

10. I.V. Stalin, *Sochineniya*, v. 12, p. 79.

families everything they need, then the collective farm cannot undertake to satisfy both social and personal needs. Then it is better to define some work as social and other work as personal. It is better to admit directly, candidly, and honestly that the collective farmer must have his own personal plot, not large, but personal. It is better to start from the fact that there is a collective economy that is public, large, dominant, and necessary to satisfy public needs; and alongside it a small, private economy, necessary to satisfy the personal needs of the collective farmer."[11]

Kind-hearted Stalin who decided that the farm family should not die of starvation in the 1930s, and just as Brezhnev who persistently urged the peasants to intensify labor on their individual plots in the 1970s naturally did not specify what part of the day peasants should devote to their "personal" economy. Obviously, only what part is left over from their work on the collective farm. This is the beginning of the black market. Here, and not at the market gates. It begins with the fact that the peasants are compelled to sell their overtime labor to society, while their labor on the collective farm is taken without payment — or almost without payment — and does not satisfy the elementary needs of the peasant family. This is the most important "transaction" in the black market; not carrots or parsley, but the life and labor of the peasant.

But who benefits from all this?

---

11. Second All-Union Congress, *op. cit.*, p. 1.

Chapter IV

The harmonious collective-farm system suits the ruling structure and is supported by it in every way because it is the ideal system for exploiting the peasant, supported in its every aspect, including the institution of personal farming.

Is it appropriate, however, to use the term *exploitation* with respect to this farming? Is the peasant not working for himself? Does he not get to keep everything he raises?

I know of a man who volunteered to relinquish his plot. And not just anywhere, but in cucumber-rich Posady, the envy of all the surrounding villages and hamlets. There in the office of the collective farm I was shown the following document:

To the management of the "Happy
Life" collective farm, from machine-
operator Tyukin, Gavrila Ivanovich.

APPLICATION
I request that our family be relieved of
its individual plot and that my wife and I
be permitted to earn on the collective farm
the additional three thousand rubles that

we receive annually at the market from the sale of early cucumbers. My request is necessitated by the fact that when my wife, Tyukin, Anna (b. 1951), was returning from work on the farm yesterday she saw colored spots before her eyes — which means she had burned herself out. When my wife stood still, the spots disappeared, but when she started working again, they came back. I attach a certificate from the medic.

In the event that my request is denied, I will forbid my wife to go to the farm, where she works as a milkmaid and seldom makes more than a hundred rubles a month. She can just work on the cucumber plot and look after the children . . .

Signed: Tyukin

The cunning Tyukin was not mistaken in his calculations: of course they did not take away his plot. The wife's earnings from the farm made no significant contribution to the family income; at any rate, her efforts in the "cucumber business" were much more rewarding. As for participation on the collective farm — as we know, it entitles a person to a personal plot — Tyukin figured that his own share of collective-farm work was great enough that his wife's health need not be sacrificed. But between work on the collective farm and at home, he never had a moment's rest.

Gratifying though the peasant's income from the individual plot may be, we must ask whether the fact that in an industrially-developed country a healthy person has to work to his physical limit (or fail to feed his family), does not signify an unnatural extension of *overtime*. Does this not amount to exorbitant exploitation?

Surplus labor creates a surplus product. This product which is taken by the ruling structure and spent on expanded production in the interests of political stability, technical-scientific research and development (in the interests of the same), and the support of people who are not active in the productive sphere, but whose activities support the existing system.

It would not be so bad if the governing party bureaucracy only took from the peasant the surplus produced on the collective farms, and left them with that product necessary for their sustenance. Then it would be acting according to the laws of commodity production. The tragedy is that both the surplus and the "necessary" product are taken.

The "proletarian" government abandoned the peasant to his fate at the very inception of widespread collectivization — during the early days of the collective farm system. Everything belonging to the peasant was whisked away, the basic necessities of life. How sadistic it was, when the XVIII party congress proudly announced, as if it were an achievement (wasn't this what they had in mind all along?), that "the average grain yield of the peasant yard in *grain-growing regions* increased from 2169 pounds in 1933 to 5184 pounds in 1937."[12] And this was on the Kuban, the Don and in Novorussia — the richest lands, which Sismondi, a hundred years before, knew to be capable not only of feeding their inhabitants, but of also

---

12. I.V. Stalin, *Voprosy leninizma*, 2nd ed. (GPI, 1952), p. 626.

"supplying all the markets left open to Russia and Poland by the civilized Europe."[13] For a large peasant family, 2169 pounds spells hunger: the prison ration plus 200 grams per person per day. And 5184 pounds is bare subsistence. And this is in grain-producing regions. Not a word about Ryazan or Smolensk, Vladimir or Vologda. As if these lands had died out. And it came close to that . . . The famine in '33. The hungry war years. Famine in '47. Famine in '49. In the other years, people did not bake grass, but they never ate their fill. As late as 1963, there were still thousands of collective farms where in a year the peasants received 200 or 250 pounds of grain and 10 to 15 rubles for their labor.[14]

The government robs the peasant of the fruits of his labor on the collective farm, but not directly, not crudely, not by physical pressure — which might provoke undesirable opposition — but surreptitiously, through a system for purchase prices. This creates the impression that the product is not taken, but bought, and the peasant who earned nothing is the one who produced little — so who's to blame?

In financing agricultural production, the authorities assume the role of a kind uncle whose extraordinary generosity moves him to back an unprofitable enterprise. But can people possibly consider it unprofitable to feed themselves?! Meat, milk and potatoes are scarce — could their production be unprofitable anywhere else? This hungry masquerade has but one purpose: to hide the

13. J. Simonde de Sismondi, *Novye nachala politicheskoy ekonomii* (Moscow, 1936), pp. 269-70.

14. See, for example, *Kollektiv kolkhoznikov, Sotsial'no-psikhologicheskoe issledovanie* (Moscow, 1970), p. 110.

obvious fact that a significant part of agricultural production is simply taken without payment, because the current prices in no way reflect its actual value.

In discussing concrete economic problems, specialists are compelled to reveal more than is usually acceptable, even if they do not reveal everything.

"Figures based on the calculation of labor expenditures in branches of material production and labor reductions caused by differences in socially-indispensable expenditure of labor on training a labor force of varied qualifications, reveal that in 1969 agriculture produced 29.4%, in 1970 28% of the national product. Furthermore, agriculture's share of the national product, as calculated by us, is higher than that indicated by current prices as determined by the Central Statistical Administration of the USSR. The latter comprised 19.5% in 1969 and 21.8% in 1970."[15]

That is, produce worth at least 30 billion rubles is taken from agriculture without recompense. Some of it is channeled back wrapped in demagoguery, but far from all, and certainly not where desired by consumers experiencing shortages of meat, dairy products, vegetables, and eggs. For many years, livestock production received such paltry returns that they barely sufficed to keep production going. As a result, even today the country suffers from a catastrophic shortage of meat, whose main victims are industrial workers, the very proletariat whose interests are supposedly at the heart of government policy.

But if livestock production is underfunded, so are the

---

15. A.P. Plotnikov, *Otnosheniya selskogo khozyaistva s pererabatyvayushchey promyshlennost'yu i torgovley* (Moscow, 1972), p. 51.

peasants engaged in livestock production, since the system of quotas and prices is such that a significant proportion of socially-indispensable labor remains unpaid. The portion of the necessary product which is extracted from the peasants free of charge is variously estimated to comprise from 40 to 60 percent of the reproduction value of moderately skilled labor. This means that from 60 to 40 percent of the peasants' necessary product must be squeezed from their personal plots.

But that is not the end. "Comparison of the actual minimum level of income of the collective-farm family with the estimated minimum of material sustenance shows that in the years 1969-70 the minimal payment of labor in the collective farms, *including all other sources of family income* was about 80 to 85 percent of the level of compensation of unskilled workers in industry."[16] Remember the thousands the peasant makes through private farming? Where are they? Why, they hardly make up for the money left unpaid by the collective farm and taken away by the government.

It would seem that a peasantry robbed in this way would be doomed to degradation and extinction. But the survival instinct is strong. Even a kitten is hard to drown, and we are dealing here with human beings. Soviet economic policy relies on this. The peasants fought on, learning to live on an acre, half an acre, fifteen square meters of land. They hang on. They struggle along, even until they have spots before their eyes. Deprived of the necessities on the collective farm, they procure them on personal plots.

---

16. M.I. Sidorova, *Vozmeshchenie neobkhodimykh zatrat i formirovanie fonda vosproizvodstva rabochey sily v kolkhozakh* (Moscow, 1972), p. 187.

Note also that after robbing the peasant on the collective farm, after squeezing him dry in the press of public socialist planning, the authorities release him into the system of market relations to recover. They release him, but reign him in with a whole series of restrictions and taboos.

The miniscule size of the personal plot and the attendant compulsory labor on a collective or state farm, strict control over foraging, lack of agricultural equipment, prohibitions on intensive use of the land, a strict prohibition on private partnerships and cooperatives — all this prevents the peasant from becoming an independent operator. This thick web of prohibitions prevents the market from developing to full strength, and prevents the formation of a direct link between production and consumer demand. The black market remains under the control of administrative authority, which dictates harsh conditions of constant exploitation of the peasant on the collective farm, the state farm, and on the individual parcel.

But at the same time, the authorities cannot, will not, and are afraid to completely proletarianize the peasant — thus making him just a hired hand. At the end of the 1960s in Latvia, the local party organs — apparently departing somewhat in the European direction from Moscow's methods of management — introduced compensation to collective farmers for renouncing their personal plots. Not much, in all 300 to 400 rubles per year; but here the amount is not the point.[17] It would appear quite logical; the collective farm receives addi-

---

17. A. S. Stamkulov, *Priusadebnoe zemlepol'zovanie* (Alma-Ata, 1972).

tional land, its earnings increase, and some compensation is paid to those who gave up the land. But no, the authorities do not need a rural proletariat; the party bureaucracy cannot utilize its labor properly, cannot create conditions whereby labor obtains the necessary product in the form of a salary, while producing a surplus product sufficient for society. The authorities can neither organize the production of goods nor market them. They can only *take* what is already produced. But what can be had from a prole? Less, at any rate, than from a peasant.

Furthermore, industrial workers have inalienable rights which, in the case of the peasantry, are quite problematic: the right to a job, a vacation, housing. (Rights that are guaranteed to some extent or other, depending on the level of development of the productive forces.) And also, of course, the right to an eight-hour work day which, though violated right and left, is still promulgated so that its violation must be justified. But in the countryside, such rights simply cannot exist. The peasant in many cases would like to be a proletarian! "According to social research, in the collective farms of the non-black-earth zone, the time spent each year by the able-bodied man engaged in collective production averaged 2600 hours, while the collective-farm woman spent 2380 hours, against the 2000 hours of optimally possible time in industrial production."[18] Adding the approximately 1000 hours spent by each collective farmer on his personal plot, we get some idea of the real expenditure of work time.

A proletarian can be made to work ten, twelve, or four-

---

18. V.I. Staroverov, *Gorod i derevnya* (Politizdat, 1972), p. 80.

teen hours a day, as is done in Soviet industrial enterprises during the monthly or quarterly rush, or towards the end of the year. But a proletarian cannot be denied wages altogether and made to provide for himself on the side. He would have nowhere to turn. If the authorities dared to regularly underpay industrial workers by 40 to 60 percent, they would be putting the very existence of the state at risk. This is why Soviet wage and price structures and distribution policies are designed to guarantee that the worker always receives a subsistence wage, even if this or that branch of industry or construction is unprofitable and the deficit has to be made up through an equivalent redistribution of the social product.

Such is the case with housing construction, for example. The authorities attempt somehow to compensate the population for the colossal housing shortage by charging low rents, which fall far short of covering construction costs, including labor. (Of course, when undercharging for housing, they pay insufficient wages, and increase the ratio of exploitation. The government gives us nothing for free.)

Indifference towards the rural worker comes so naturally to the authorities that they do not even bother to disguise it very carefully. They can pay him as little as they like, without regard for any social norms. If he supplements it on the black market and personal plot, this is no threat to the government and party bureaucracy. On the contrary, though ostensibly condemning market relations, the authorities in fact push the peasant onto the market with the products of household plots, and a significant part of social needs are satisfied in this way. Where else would it come from? How can needs and possibilities be balanced? How can a head-on collision between the interests of society and those of the party bureaucracy be averted? Only in theoretical tracts does planned socialism run smoothly without the marketplace; in real life it jams.

I do not know whether anyone in Latvia managed to get 300 rubles for giving up his land, or whether anyone at all chose to sell himself into bondage in this way. But you can be sure that the initiators of this measure received party reprimands, and it serves them right. It doesn't do to betray your own interests, chop off your own perch: things will grind to a halt without personal plots and the market.

The peasant is forced to put in two days' work every day. Most of what he earns on the first day, in the *Kolkhoz*, in the public socialist system, is confiscated by the government and redistributed in the interests of preserving the existing system. The peasant is left with neither the necessary product nor the right to use the surplus. Then begins the second day, according to the law of blackmarket commodity production, of *private* socialism — a working day during which the peasant invests all his personal capital: his own labor (what is left over from collective labor) and that of his family. He determines the level of exploitation here. The minimum is enough to ward off starvation; the maximum is just short of the point of collapse from lack of sleep, working from three in the morning to ten at night. He determines the nature of production (within permitted bounds), depending on the demand for this or that product.

We know that a significant proportion of the produce of the personal plots — from 20 to 90 percent — is realized.

The peasant's income depends on the margin of profit. But profit is part of surplus value, which is created in surplus time. How much surplus time is there in private farming? Here the peasant is his own workman as well as his own "capitalist."

This black-market trade is so pathetic on an individual basis, this profit margin, this average return on investment, this surplus time, seem so comical to serious economists that they do not bother to study it. Or perhaps they turn aside deliberately, so as not to see the obvious truth that our socialism lives off black-market "microcapitalism." When they do acknowledge it, they try to tone down its impact. They say that the "time" spent by collective farmers on individual farming cannot be called working time or a second work-day. This is "non-working time necessary to conduct subsidiary farming."[19] What idiocy! "Non-working time," when it provides half the family's total income! While we feed ourselves with products produced by the peasant playing around in his "non-working" time.

Just lately, however, importunate reality has forced a closer look at the village, revealing fragments of the real picture. "We share the view that when the personal plot becomes a principal source of income and is basically market-oriented while the work of a member of a peasant family in the socialized economy serves only as a means to obtain the right to run an operation, the latter can be regarded as a small private enterprise," writes a Soviet sociologist.[20] To admit the existence of small *private* enter-

19. Baykova *et al.*, *Svobodnoe vremya i vsestoronnee razvitie lichnosti* (Moscow, 1965), p. 237.

20. V.I. Staroverov, "Preodolenie sushchestvennykh razlichiy mezhdu

prises in the land of developed socialism is no mean feat. Such an admission cannot help but call forth re-examination from top to bottom (or from bottom to top) of the entire system of economic relations. To admit to the existence of 40 million small private enterprises after almost half a century of collectivization is to admit also to the complete *economic* inefficiency of the collective farm system. But then it must be conceded that the collective farms are politically very useful since, co-existing as they do with small private enterprise, they create ideal conditions for robbing the peasantry with the help of the black market.

Alas, after making an all-but-revolutionary "discovery," that same sociologists after a few generalities also claims that the peasant economy "will voluntarily wither away as the public economy develops. Guaranteeing the conditions for the disappearance of that economy as a source of supplementary earnings will make it possible to eliminate the residual backwardness of the countryside when compared to the city."[21]

No, private farming will not wither away, voluntarily or otherwise! As leading specialists have noted, for the collective and state farms in the year 2000 to completely satisfy the mounting needs of society in basic foodstuffs and take the place of private farms of peasants and workers, the production of meat would have to increase 4.5 times; milk, 3 times; eggs, 8 times. And this is not all. The problem goes beyond economics. Such rapid growth of agriculture might perhaps be possible if the system of

gorodom i derevney kak sostavnaya chast' postroeniya sotsial'no odnorod-nogo obshchestva," in *Sotsiologicheskie issledovaniya*, 1975, p. 51.

    21. *Ibid.*

prohibitions and restrictions on economic resourceful-ness were relaxed. But no, personal peasant plots will live on in their present form as long as the ruling structure achieves its policy by means of the black market. Whether its policy can be maintained by any other means is very doubtful, but the possibility ought to be investigated.

The peasant is not to blame for the fact that he has to carry on market production on a parcel the size of a child's sandbox. If we want to understand what kind of society we live in, we have no right to turn our backs on him. Particularly because the games played out on these toy parcels are far from childish in their cruelty.

Chapter V

The domino players who rattle the ivories in city yards, squares and boulevards are not to be seen on village streets, either in the evening or on holidays. In the country, idleness is considered shameful. Even city domino players do not take their board games with them when they visit their native villages. They arrange for leave during the summer haymaking, or the fall potato harvest, so that they an help their parents or family with the farm work. People who live in the country never get a break from work; they are self-employed, after all, and who would take over? Who will make up the loss, if the cucumbers are not watered or the potatoes not dug? You can't cut grass in winter. Feeding, watering, milking and tending the herd does not leave much time for dominoes.

Before and after work on the *kolkhoz*, machine-operator Tyukin stubbornly works to obtain what he has been denied by the *kolkhoz* treasury. Steadily he goes about his business, moving from one task to the next, with axe, scythe or shovel. And he is not alone; all of his family, led by Nyurka, works alongside. He seems to be an attentive father to his children: if his wife is ill, he himself sees them off to school, cooks their meals, checks their clothes for rips. He is a tender, loving husband to his Nyurka. He is a faithful son to his old parents; it was for their sake, so as not desert them in their feeble old age, that he became a collective farmer when he got out of the army, instead of going off to build communism. But despite all this, he cannot free any of them from the unending toil of the peasant — not the ailing old folks, not his wife until just before she gives birth, and not the children. Even were he to do so, conscience would forbid them to shirk while the rest of the family was working in the orchard or meadow. They could never make ends meet without the conscientious participation of everyone in the family.

Can two adults working on a collective or state farm also work their personal holding effectively enough to feed a family of five or six people? The answer is no. To obtain a potato harvest from an acre-sized plot, two able-bodied people must put in a full work day two months at a stretch.[22] A cow takes one-and-a-half to two hours daily; and all the other livestock also requires time and attention. And no one releases the peasant from work on the collective farm, especially not in summer. [23] But in those

----

22. According to the estimates of the Government Planning committee (Gosplan) of the USSR, it takes 2.8 man-days of labor on the personal plot to produce a hundred kilos of potatoes (*Izvestiya*, Jan. 14, 1977). An acre-sized plot yields about 5,000 kilos. Under the very favorable conditions of the Khmel'nitsk region it takes 3 man-days on the personal plot to produce 100 kilos of milk, 45.5 man-days per head of cattle. See V.A. Belyaev, *Lichnoe podsobnoe khozyaystvo pri sotsializme* (Ekonomika, 1970), p. 95.

23. In the Novosibirsk region, which is not outstanding among the agricultural regions of the country and can very well be taken as the statistical median, "the average length of the work-day (on collective and state farms — L.T.) increased from 7.8 to 8.4 hours in winter, and from 8 to 9 hours in summer between 1967 and 1972, according to workers. The percentage of people working 8 to 11 hours went from 30 to 55%; the percentage of people working

same summer months the hay must be brought in for the winter and all the other chores still have to be done. No, two people would have neither the strength nor the time. In large families, those who earn the right to personal farming — collective farmers and state-farm workers —are not the main workers in their own gardens.

The personal plot system is a colossal exploiter of children, the aged, and the invalid. There are twelve million rural inhabitants who work nowhere but on these plots, of whom seven-and-a-half million are aged or adolescent.[24] The rest are mainly disabled or partially unfit for work or mothers of large families. Add another 15 million rural children — the number of school-age children not counting those in primary school — and you begin to see who is largely responsible for the gross agricultural product which literally and figuratively feeds the government in the land of developed socialism, with its powerful party-government and ideological apparatus.[25]

The exploitation of the young and unfit, glossed over by sociologists and economists, can be inferred from the

---

more than 12 hours doubled. Only a third of the workers in 1972 had a normal working day, while the remaining two-thirds worked overtime to a greater or lesser degree." R.V. Ryvkina, "K izucheniyu osnovnykh napravleniy urbanizatsii obraza zhizni sel'skogo naseleniya," in *Sovremennaya sibirskaya derevnya* (Novosibirsk, 1975), part 1, p. 36.

24. Belyaev, *op. cit.*, pp. 81, 93.

25. "Developed socialism of this kind has its roots in "ancient history": the linguistic facts reveal that the ancient source of slavery is connected with family law. The word *semiya* (according to Vostokov's dictionary) means slaves, household servants. The terms *rab* (slave) — *robya, robenets, rebenik* — and *kholop* (in Ukrainian *khlopets*, meaning boy, son) referred to people subject to paternal authority as well as to slaves. M.F. Vladimirskiy-Budanov, *Obzor istorii russkogo prava.* Cited in B.D. Grekov, *Krest'yane na Rusi*, p. 132.

writings of lawyers, who have to precisely define the legal aspect of rural family relationships. "The family of the collective farmer, in contradistinction to that of the worker in industry or service, is characterized by the existence not only of blood and marriage ties, . . . but also of definite labor relations uniting the individuals as a consequence of their mutual maintenance of a personal plot."[26]

A more precise definition is in order: the peasant's family is a micro-capitalist enterprise where the head of the family is required to exploit the labor of all its members in order to obtain maximum surplus value from the personal plot and so make up for the necessary product not received on the collective or state farm. This exploitation is carried on, as a rule, by completely barbaric methods, without any labor-saving devices, without machines, without the application of modern techniques of agronomy and animal husbandry. Spade, wheel-barrow, sack, basket — these are almost the only tools. At best, a collective-farm tractor driver might plow and harrow the plot for a couple of bottles of vodka. Everything else is done by hand.

One magniloquent party babbler declared that "the farming operation of the rural family has changed radically in the Soviet period. Now there is no need to worry about the tools of production, the horse, the fertility of soil."[27] True enough, the horse is no problem nowadays. Nowadays people pull their own load. The slogan "the horse is a menace to socialism" was propagated as early as

---

26. *Kommentariy k primernomu Ustavu kolkhoza* (Moscow, 1972), p. 239.

27. P. Shelest, *Odna sel'skaya sem'ya (Shtrikhi k sotsial'nomu portretu sel'skogo rabochego 70-kh godov)*, (Moscow, 1972), p. 79.

the thirties. It's perfectly true that a village woman crawling on all fours, pulling a load like a horse, is no menace to socialism.

The government closed its eyes a long time ago to the peasant's method of getting his bread, which involves such severe overstrain. So what if the factories "make spades a good kilo too heavy. Rakes are also too heavy. They don't make tools for teen-agers or older people at all."[28] What a dreadful picture: children, invalids and old people and women, using shovels and rakes too heavy for them, produce on two percent of the land under cultivation almost as much as strong, healthy people in full possession of modern technology produce on the remaining ninety-eight percent. What a terrible crime is hidden in these newspaper admissions!

Notably, in the last few years the number of personal plots near cities where intensive raising of cattle takes place has increased, as has the number of greenhouses. The possibility of obtaining relatively high profits motivates these micro-capitalists to think in terms of at least micro-mechanization: converting domestic vacuum cleaners into garden sprayers, adapting mixers for gathering gooseberries, inventing equipment for growing tulips in winter.

But on the whole, private farming sticks to the tried and true. It could not be otherwise, for, in the absence of technology suited to such small-scale farming, there is only one means of increasing production, and that is by increasing labor. The labor of adults working on the collective farms cannot be increased — they would collapse. Therefore women with many children, old peo-

---

28. *Izvestiya*, Jan. 4, 1977.

ple, invalids and children are obliged to work more.

There is, of course, no division of labor, no cooperation to increase output, nor can there be. The personal plot is not land ownership, nor even leasing. The peasant's right to his individual parcel entitles him to till the land only with the help of his family. The family's work load can be eased only by resorting to the simple mutual assistance of two or three collective-farm families according to the pinciple "you scratch my back and I'll scratch yours." This is how people with small families dig potatoes, and how in some regions they carry out very simple personal construction.

But it is strictly taboo to combine these two or three peasant holdings into a more rational, intensive *market* operation. A rational division of labor and intensive market-oriented farming would reveal all too clearly the *capitalist* nature of such combinations, no longer even deserving of the prefix "micro." If even today personal plots, weighed down by prohibitions, compete successfully with collective and state farms, the most elementary combination of independent peasant enterprises would certainly demonstrate the utter irrationality of the existing collective farms. Clearly, the authorities will not take this step. The party bureaucracy will never accept even the doubling or tripling of the food production as sufficient cause for a further development of personal plots. The political rationale for this prohibition is simple: by preserving "developed" socialism — a situation of semi-starvation but of unconditional party-bureaucracy rule — by preserving the black market, they prevent the development of open-market relations, which have very little need of any administration.

In general, any *voluntary* association of private people in the countryside, independent of collective- or state-farm administration, is impossible, no matter whether it is capitalist or communist in nature. In a country advertising itself as a model of the initial states of communism, *communes* are absolutely forbidden. They already existed under the Czar and in the first years of Soviet rule, but disappeared with the onset of collectivization. Stalin buried them personally. "Only as the strengthening and consolidation of agricultural collectives progress can the ground be laid for the mass movement of peasants toward the commune. However, that will not be soon. Therefore the commune, representing the highest form of development, can be the center of the collective-farm movement only in the future . . ."[29] It did not matter to him where he sent his victims — to the past or to the future —as long as it was to non-existence (lest they interfere with the present).

The communards were people religiously committed to the communist idea. Such cohesive, committed collectives could and did offer serious resistance to the Soviet policy of coercing the peasantry into serfdom. "A certain number of the communes displayed an anti-governmental attitude manifested by contrasting the commune's interests with those of the government (an excessive increase in the consumption of the commune, diminished production of public commodities, etc.)."[30] So that was it! The communards did not want to become

---

29. I.V. Stalin, "Otvet tovarishcham kolkhoznikam," *Voprosy leninizma,* 2nd ed., p. 351.

30. *Great Soviet Encyclopedia,* 1st ed., v. 33. "Kommuna sel'skokhozya-istvennaya."

beasts of burden with a subhuman standard of living, working their strip of land under the whip of the party bureaucracy. So they were put under collective farm regulation, and then made to drive their children and old folks out to work.[31]

Exploitation of the peasant family as a single economic unit has turned out to be so convenient that lately it occurs not only through the head of the family on the individual parcel, but right on the collective farm. For instance, in Chuvashia (I happened to see this in Chuvashia, but informed sources confirm that it is almost ubiquitous) the potato fields are divided into plots, and each peasant family is assigned to harvest potatoes from a plot whose size depends on the number of souls on hand. Only the fulfillment of this corvee labor (which does not, of course, bring release from other work) confers the right to buy feed at the *kolkhoz* for one's own cattle and the right to undisputed use of the personal plot.

The number of souls on hand in the family is calculated according to the direct, mystical meaning of the word; as long as the soul is still in the body, it counts. Only paralytics are exempted. At least, on the collective farm in

---

31. It is not only in the countryside, and not only economic cooperation between people which is impossible. For example, an unsuccessful struggle has been going on between young people and party authorities over the question of "interest clubs," representing, if not the intensification of social activity, then at least the intensification of social thought and life. Such clubs are permitted only under the constant, petty scrutiny of komsomol officials. But it is difficult to maintain such clubs even within this prescribed ideological-fiscal system, given the pressures; the young people move towards independence of thought, and the clubs are disbanded and their organizers are subjected to ideological and sometimes even administrative repressions. It stands to reason that economic cooperation would be even harder to sustain under these conditions.

Chuvashia, "Kanashsky," no exemptions were granted in assigning this work to a blind man and his wife.

This *kolkhoz*, I might point out, is one of the leading lights in the country. There are only five or six like it in any region, and they are presented in newspaper and magazine articles as a socialist achievement. This is where they invite journalists. Machine-operators and dairy-maids earn more there than on neighboring collective farms. But who bothers to look behind the billboard smiles at the labors and tears beneath the surface?

The director of the "Kanashsky" *kolkhoz* is an effective manager, an agronomist of merit, holder of the orders of Lenin and the Octobor Revolution, and author of a book, "Land and Harvest." One must suppose that he did not invent this system, but he uses it successfully. How many such enlightened serf-holders are there? People ought to know every one by name, perhaps then they would be ashamed. Or would they? The district party committee would absolve them of their sins.

In some places sugar beets and fodder crops are harvested in this way. It is important to note that this barbaric system of work cannot offer the peasant even a pretense of material incentive; this is merely a way of brutalizing the conditions for acquiring the right to a personal plot.

The psychological factors behind this kind of work pattern were well known to Marx, and to Fourier before him: "women do good work only under male supervision, but . . . on the other hand, women and children are zealous in exerting themselves once they have undertaken a task, whereas the adult male worker is crafty enough to conserve his energy as much as possible."[32]

---

32. K. Marx, *Kapital*, v. 1 (Gospolitizdat, 1963), p. 707.

In Central Asia girls of twelve or fourteen (for some reason, I found these to be mostly girls) are made to loosen the soil of the collective-farm cotton fields with heavy hoes — one or two kilos heavier than the norm. They work long hours in the hot sun, instead of going to school, or sometimes even after school. This work may actually be harder than the gathering of potatoes from the autumn mud so familiar to the children of central Russia.

One of the schoolteachers in Gati (the central Russian village where Aksinya Egoryevna lived and died) had doubts about including farming lessons into the school curriculum. It seemed to her that the children already knew this subject quite well. So she sent questionnaires to the pupils, and passed the results along to her superiors. All the children answered that they worked *three* times on the potato harvest: once at home, again on the collective-farm field with their family, and finally, on the collective-farm field with their class. At haymaking they worked *twice*: first with their family for the forestry collective or some other organization that had land and would pay a little something, and then for the collective farm for the "ten percent," the right to one-tenth of the hay gathered. Then there were all the other chores: work on the personal plot in spring, summer and fall, and year-round care of livestock — that last predominately a girl's job.

Her superiors studied the questionnaires with care, but went ahead and announced the introduction of lessons in farming. Not because they were needed, but because a higher authority requested it. The highest authority of all, the one possessed only of humanitarian considerations, had issued instructions forbidding child labor in the fields. And now it was concerned, from the same humanitarian impulse, that rural children not become lazy and grow up to be shirkers.

But the exalted ministerial authorities are distant, while the district party and economic officials are close at hand. And they could not get the harvest in, the soil raked, or the feed prepared without child labor. Are the ministerial authorities, with their humanitarian decrees, aware of this? Of course they are, but their business as bureaucrats is to issue humanitarian decrees. And the business of the local educational authorities is to follow orders, those from Moscow as well as those coming from the district party committee. As a result, peasant children, already three times exploited, must work a fourth time as a *lesson* in farming. In this case their exploiters are humanitarian educational authorities whose dividends come not in the form of potatoes or good marks in the economic plan, but in good marks in the pedagogical plan.

The economic necessity of working on the personal plot has existed for many years, and this has influenced the moral climate of rural life, eventually hardening into custom, into moral doctrine. Custom in turn dictates a certain way of behaving, taking advantage of man's moral pliancy. Still, exploitation by any other name remains exploitation.

The teacher from Gati used to complain of her enormous difficulties every spring and fall, when garden work would begin. She had no time, energy or desire to plant and dig potatoes. Hers was a family of two — herself and her husband. Both had been working for twenty-five years in the school; they devoted all their time and thought to it. They had no need whatever of a potato patch, since they earned enough to buy produce. Nevertheless, every year they planted, and worked the potatoes. They did it for the sole reason that *everyone in the village does it*. If they tried to give up their garden, it would be interpreted in the village as eccentricity or — even worse — snobbery. "How could you give your land up of your own free will?" You do not buy potatoes if you can grow them yourself. In the village you have to live like everybody else, even though you may have ideas of your own. Economic uniformity leads to moral uniformity. Established patterns come to seem natural and inevitable.

But material factors are even more to the point here; most teachers cannot buy any produce from the collective farm or from the villagers, since they specialize in one commercial crop, producing only enough of other products for their members' personal use. So teachers are forced to farm alongside the peasants. Agricultural specialists — agronomists, experts in animal husbandry, engineers — suffer less from this lack of produce, but they are also affected to some extent. "Personal plots are particularly essential in the peculiar conditions of the sheep-raising state farms of Kazakhstan, which are located in sparsely-populated regions far from large cities and rail links. A survey of twelve such farms revealed that all specialists' families kept cows and sheep, and some also kept camels and mares for koumiss."[33]

Circumstances make this necessary. Circumstances determine the way of life. They determine behavior. And thoughts. People are not born slaves. They come under

---

33. I.V. Makarova, *Lichnoe podsobnoe khozyaystvo sel-skogo naseleniya v perspektinom ekonomicheskom i sotsial'nom planirovanii.* Tselinograd, 1975.

the sway of conformity and blind necessity only when they enter school, and even then the process is gradual. While they are still learning to write, their distinctive handwriting still shows through. But beginning in the second grade, the children start asking in the school library for "something about Lenin — because they told us to read it." This is the beginning of conformist thinking. It is increased by common work obligations: beginning in the fourth grade, the children work in the *kolkhoz* fields and in their personal plots. Word and deed reinforce one another. Thus is the human being formed . . . and his own words are enough to make you scream from frustration.

From the homework of Grigori Galkin, a fifth-grader from Gati:

A LETTER TO MY FRIEND

My dear friend Vasya!

I will describe to you my free day. I got up early, washed, dressed, and helped my mother make the beds. Then I sat down to breakfast, had breakfast, and we went to dig potatoes. I dug, and my sister picked them up. It was cold. My sister got a little frozen, and so did I. We dug for a while. We got tired and had a rest. Then we dug potatoes. We warmed up. Suddenly we hear mom: "Dinner time!" And we went and had dinner. Then we went to dig potatoes. After dinner the time flew by fast. It was evening already. We had something to eat. And we went to bed. That's how my day went. Tell me about your day, Vasya.

Your friend Grinya

In our childhood, my schoolmates and I used to declaim, "Thank you, comrade Stalin, for our happy childhood." Who should today's rural children thank?

Chapter VI

"Thank God for Lenin," said Aksinya Egoryevna one day, gazing at his portrait in the local newspaper. "He has a kind face, he took care of us." Another time, already without surprise, I saw her bow to the same portrait in the new village council building. "May you rest in peace. What a life you gave us — a pension, and a garden, coffee and tea at the shop — it's a shame to leave such a life."

Everyone knows that we owe life today to Lenin. We live by his legacy. And anyone can see that the life of today's peasant is incomparably better than it was in the thirties, forties and fifties. The work is hard? But the work was hard in those days too, and life was worse. Who does not remember how miserably people lived even in the early sixties, when the collective farms paid nothing and personal holdings were cut?

And now? Having long since forgotten how the peasant *might* live, we remember well that not so long ago he lived as nobody should or could live. All memory of the NEP period, not to mention prerevolutionary times, has faded from popular consciousness (the truth is banned, and lies do not convince), but people remember well the hard labor of the collective farms in the worst years. Well-being is measured in relation to that dead point. Deprived of history, the experience of his ancestors and knowledge of what life can be, the peasant can only compare the present with the worst years of his own life and say, "It's not so bad, we are managing!"

We, city people, judge peasant life entirely on the basis of images thrust upon us by newspapers, magazines and carefully-filmed, painstakingly-assembled television programs. Together with impressions picked up at the market: "At the Cheremushki market they're selling veal for seven rubles! These peasants have the nerve! What do they do with their money?" And I am again reminded of the post-war sack of money that struck my imagination as a child. Surely now the sack truly holds an even hundred thousand.

No one could fail to observe that life has become easier, the noose has loosened. There is no devastating famine today, no peasants beg in the streets of the city. They do not swell up from hunger, nor do they manage on potatoes only. But let us look closely at today's rural plenty, at the peasant's daily life, his expenditures and economies. Knowing how the peasants work, let us see how they reap the fruit of their labor.

They save money — not the famous sack, of course, but enough for an emergency. They amass grain; bread was first sold in the countryside a mere ten years ago, and if hard times should come again the peasant would be the first to suffer. And bread and potatoes are the main foods. They lay aside some slate, which is hard to get hold of when the roof needs repairing. Our Aksinya Egoryevna had a barrel of salt in store. I really don't know why. Salt is the one thing always for sale. Perhaps there was a shortage during the war? I was somehow embarrassed to ask, and in any case, she would have avoided talking about her reserves. Salt is essential. An urban family might pickle cabbage or cucumbers, but ony for pleasure, because home-made is better than store-bought. Peasants cannot buy anything of the sort. They have to make it at home, or else go without pickles; but without them the everpresent potatoes don't taste right.

A city dweller can buy a pillow in a store. Peasants save down for years to make one. The thriftier the housewife, the heavier her pillows and featherbeds. But all this takes much time and effort. Housework and home-production are an inalienable extension of personal plots. This work is essential, and takes up as much time (especially women's time) as the garden and livestock — an average of three hours a day. Where does the energy come from?[34]

The individual plot is a life-or-death matter to the peasant. Drought is a *personal* tragedy for him; feed for the cattle has to be found somewhere, even if only one blade of grass at a time. The Colorado beetle, imported from Poland along with seed potatoes by careless bureaucrats, is a *personal* tragedy for him; he has to get down on all fours and collect them in a jar of kerosene. Cattle disease is a personal tragedy; if a yearling steer, ready for market, dies, the peasent mourns him as if some relative had passed away.

---

34. "52.9% of the people studied averaged more than 5 hours a day on their personal plots. Two-thirds of them were women. 49.4% of the men studied and 47.3% of the women worked on the personal plots every day of the week. Exactly half of the people who spent from 2 to 5 hours on the personal plot were men." V.T. Kolokol'nikova, "Brachno-semeynye otnosheniya v srede kolkhoznogo krest'yanstva," *Sotsiologicheskie issledovaniya,* no. 3, 1976, p. 84.

Not every emergency can be anticipated, but you have to have at least a little of everything stored up.

The worst thing that can happen is for the peasant himself to fall ill. How can you get sick-leave on your own plot? You get your pennies from the *kolkhoz*, of course, and thank heavens for that — they didn't pay a thing before 1964. But if collective-farm wages are low to begin with, what can you say about the percentage paid to the sick? Even the sick have to fend for themselves.

Aksinya Egoryevna had been complaining for a long time that she was in such pain *it hurt to lie down*, but when she was called to the timber collective to clear a swamp for a few kopecks, she not only went, she went running. She bought a bottle for a forester she knew to thank him for the invitation. What's the good of health in winter if you can't get hold of any hay?

The old-age pension is twenty rubles. A person cannot live on twenty rubles, even by going hungry. But as a favor they leave a sixty-year-old woman her personal parcel. It's all yours, old-timer, break your back, maybe you'll manage to make a little something. Besides, the country needs your potatoes, your work is essential. The socialist fatherland is threatened by famine. If you have the strength to work the land yourself, then ask your children from the city to help. They can take leave, or else simply play truant from work, but they'll come somehow and help out; the potatoes are important to them too. You won't sit idly by either, of course.

If anyone is so blind as not to see that the peasant puts in *two work-days* every twenty-four hours (on the collective farm and on his own personal parcel), he has only to look at the old people of the village. They are left with just one work-day, but only because they have been released from the *kolkhoz* corvée. The authorities are indifferent to the fate of these old people, and they know it. But who doesn't think of himself? It can be frightening to look old age and illness in the face. Some pretty terrible sights stare back at you. As long as you can, you want to keep putting aside another ten rubles, just in case. So that the peasant's bag of money turns out the beggar's hat — not a hundred thousand rubles, but bare sustenance for a rainy day. To save up this bare minimum, the peasant has to cut down on his alredy scant daily needs, cut family requirements to a primitive level.[35]

I am aware that it is imprecise to say that the "peasant has to cut down on his needs." Needs are not subject to willpower, and if Aksinya Egoryevna said that she didn't care for tea, then she had no need of it. But these subtleties of definition are not important. Everyone likes meat, of course, but even official data shows that a rural inhabitant receives scarcely more than a hundred grams of meat and lard a day. Considering that the peasant is even less likely to use butter than Aksinya Egoryevna is to use tea; and considering, to put it bluntly if inelegantly, that lard is the basic fat in the peasant diet (used to fry

---

35. "The small producer forces his children to work at an earlier age, works longer hours, lives more 'frugally,' and reduces his personal needs to the point where he is considered a barbarian in civilized countries." Here Lenin (*Sochineniya*, 3rd ed., v. 2, pp. 468-69) is providing a commentary to Kautsky and Marx. Much of what Kautsky wrote a hundred years ago about the West European peasantry, especially about small farms, is applicable today to the Soviet socialist peasantry, which has not been raised above the level of the remote past. It was a line of Kautsky's that provided me with the title of this work: "The peasant's art of starving can lead to the economic excellence of small production."

potatoes, make cabbage soup); and considering that far more than a hundred grams of meat is eaten during the four or five holiday feasts — nothing remains of the daily portion. But did that daily portion really exist in the first place?

Official statistics apparently exist for the sole purpose of concealing the truth. The division of peasants into collective-farm and state-farm workers helps achieve this purpose, insofar as the latter can be counted among urban blue- and white-collar workers. Suppose that per capita use of meat and lard is being measured. The result is 51 kg. in families of blue- and white-collar workers, 37 kg. in collective-farm families. But the former category includes both state-farm workers, who have no more than the collective-farm peasants, and party and upper-level government officials, whose food consumption is capped only by physiological limitations. The gap between the two groups becomes less striking, for the higher figure is factitiously depressed, but the national average remains unchanged: "What can you do, we have not yet achieved abundance, everyone suffers equally."

But this is not yet the whole story. Lately, even collective farmers have not been treated separately in statistics of food consumption. One overall figure is given — 57 kg. per capita consumption of meat and animal products in 1977, for instance — as if a collective farmer and an agricultural administrator ate the same.

What refined scoundrel gave the name "Russian *izba*" to a restaurant set up in the midst of the country houses of party big shots? Had he ever set foot in a Russian *izba*? Isn't it in manor-houses that people gorge themselves so?

According to norms established by the Nutrition Institute of the Academy of Medical Sciences, an adult should consume an average of 81 kg. of meat and fat per year to sustain normal activity. Of the long list of foods in this ideal diet, only bread and potatoes are consumed by the peasant in above-average quantities. Although, as a matter of fact, Soviet urban consumption, even as calculated by the Central Statistical Administration, also falls far short of the norm.

Meat is not only not eaten daily in the countryside, it does not even appear at the peasant table every week. The peasant and his family *have to* go without meat, *have to* satisfy their hunger with bread and cabbage, *have to* because their situation is such that there is no way to meet the most elementary requirements for clothing, housing, etc., except at the expense of equally elementary requirements for protein foods.

The deficiency of meat and animal protein affects particularly the growth of children and adolescents. Adolescent schoolchildren in rural areas are ten to twenty centimeters shorter than urban schoolchildren. No studies of differences in mental development have been published; they are hardly likely to be undertaken, for fear that reality would contradict the propaganda nonsense. As indirect evidence of damage to mental development, one can point to the fact that deaths resulting from mental disturbances are three times more frequent among rural youths aged 15-19 than among their urban counterparts.[36] These are mental disturbances resulting

---

36. M.S. Bednyy, *Prodolzhitel'nost' zhizni v gorodakh i selakh*, (Moscow, Statistika, 1976), pp. 46, 73.

in death. How many are less than fatal? How many are not serious enough to warrant consulting a doctor and submitting to the shame of registering at a psychiatric clinic (in a peasant's mind, a fate almost equal to death)?[37]

The most normal, urgent needs, brought on by the whole beggarly life of the peasant, are extraordinarily poorly met. The expectations are low. Low, the lowest of any segment of society. Suppose an urban family uses 150 liters of water daily. Try cutting off the water supply for two days in a city apartment house and telling the residents to fetch water in pails from the building next door. It would be impossible. You'd almost have a political riot. But one out of every two peasant families carries water farther than 100 meters, while some (one in ten) carry it farther than a half kilometer. They carry it by hand, of course; thanks to the authorities, the peasant doesn't have to take care of a horse, plus there is no danger to mature socialism.[38]

"According to the local Soviets data, only 17% of villages surveyed have good-quality water, in 70% the water was satisfactory, and in 13% it was salty or polluted."[39] Anyone who has ever been in the countryside knows the "satisfactory" water from the village well — a turbid suspension that leaves a one-inch deposit of mud on the bottom of the pail. But at least you can drink it, if

---

37. In the Russian province a psychiatric patient is seen as a non-person. His condition may arouse curiosity, but not pity or compassion. This is the basis for the policy of confining dissidents in psychiatric hospitals, even though they may be perfectly sane.

38. *Migratsiya sel'skogo naseleniya* (Moscow, Mysl', 1970), p. 313.

39. *Ibid.*, p. 312.

you wait for it to settle. The "polluted and salty" water cannot be disinfected or filtered, it has to be drunk as is. It's not so much that people have grown accustomed to "satisfactory" or salty water; in the majority of cases, they simply know no other.

Sanitary inspection is not the answer to the water problem. A sanitary inspector can close down a well, leaving a village completely without water. But he cannot have new wells dug or artesian wells drilled, because means and manpower are lacking, and besides, the local authorities have no interest in such construction. Most of the wells in central-Russian villages date back to the last century, and their use has not become more hygienic with time — only the framework has been renewed several times. There is no demand for change from below (the peasants "don't care for" pure water) or from above, since district administrators have no need to concern themselves with village wells, and this applies even more at the regional and national levels. They are in no hurry to allocate the funds, either.

Villages with large livestock farms are the most fortunate. Here an artesian well is usually drilled and the cattle receive water directly in feeding-bowls — the managers are made responsible for this — and people obtain water from a hydrant on the street. The water is still a long way from good, but at least it is cleaner, and people don't dip their buckets in it. Things turn out so well when private interests coincide with social interests (those of collective-farm cattle).

The organization of medical service in rural areas deserves a separate study. It is obvious, at least, that the farther one is from a hospital (that is, from a large town or district center), the more difficult it is to obtain the timely services of a qualified doctor. And although mortality is significantly higher in rural areas, peasants see a doctor two to three times less often than do city people.[40] However, people who live in small settlements far from hospitals are less dissatisfied with medical service than people in large villages.[41] A paradox? Let's see.

When Aksinya Egoryevna was too sick to lie down, instead of hitching a ride to the doctor fifteen kilometers away (or walking, if nobody gave her a lift), she went in the opposite direction — also fifteen kilometers — to clear the swampland. A visit to the doctor takes all day, and if you aren't lucky, you have to spend the night. Analysis and tests take a week. What peasant can afford this kind of "free medicine," especially in the summer? It would cost more than hiring a private doctor for a week, if such things existed.

It never entered Aksinya Egoryevna's mind that a doctor might make a house call, except that the vet might look at a sick animal for three rubles or a bottle. She had never once even called the young local medical assistant. During the last winter, when she was already dying, she continued to walk to the clinic at the opposite end of the village. It was only in the final week, when she was totally bed-ridden, that she greeted the medical assistant with a grateful, though weak, whisper, when she came to administer a shot of morphine. Aksinya Egoryevna was not one to complain of poor medical service.

What does the peasant find, if he manages to get to the

40. Bednyy, *op. cit.,* p. 31.
41. *Migratsiya sel'skogo naseleniya*, p. 298.

district town hospital? The real state of medical care is a forbidden topic. But the journal *Woman Worker* (no. 5, 1977) provides some unexpected evidence:

ASSISTANCE RENDERED. L.V. Nestrueva, of the town of Agli in the Aktyubinsk region, wrote to our journal about unsanitary conditions in the local maternity home and neglect of the patients on the part of medical personnel . . . As the editors have informed Deputy-Minister of Health of the USSR V. Ch. Novikov, these allegations concerning the organization of the maternity ward at the hospital in Agli were generally confirmed. The following measures have been effected as a result of the investigation of this complaint: maternity facilities in the town of Agli in the Aktyubinsk region have been moved to a new location and provided with hot water and essential equipment; round-the-clock presence of physicians — obstetricians/gynecologists — has been established; monitoring of the sanitary regimen of the maternity ward has been increased. L.V. Nestrueva has been provided with quality medical care.

How long did they deliver, without hot water or essential equipment, and at night without an obstetrician, in the world's most advanced country? How many such hospitals and maternity homes are there? Nearly all of them are like that. At least, I myself heard a woman tearfully relate how, in one of the Moscow maternity homes, she almost gave birth to a baby in a lavatory pan, because she couldn't rouse the sleeping attendants with her screams. So the "sanitary regimen" is unlikely to be maintained in the Agli hospital after the attention of the central authorities is withdrawn. One desperate woman complained, they "responded to the signal," but how many people know that birth, life and death could and should be different?

Aksinya Egoryevna never complained to anyone about anything at all. To complain, one has to be conscious of one's self as a separate individual personality with rights. Rights create necessities, just as urgent necessity compels a search for rights. But Aksinya Egoryevna knew no rights other than the right to her personal plot, and that only in return for working on the collective farm. Plus the right to an old-age pension of twenty rubles. That is all. These rights are firm. All other rights, to the contrary, are very, very shaky. Rural custom takes the place of a legal code for the peasant: "We live no worse than other people, and that's enough."

Klavdia Vasilyevna Yudakova, a peasant woman of Aksinya Egoryevna's age from the village of Ubory, near Moscow, used to moonlight as a cleaning woman in the club, for which she was paid ten rubles a month — a trifling sum, of course, but every little bit helps when you are raising four little girls without a husband. When the time came to calculate her pension, it was discovered that the minimum wage for a cleaning woman was at least *thirty* rubles more. Klavdia Vasilyevna was being robbed of thirty rubles a month, by the director of the collective farm. But Klavdia Vasilyevna made no complaint; nor did she seek to obtain the money she had earned by the sweat of her brow. She was grateful to have her pension based on the full amount. It is better not to mess with the management, you never win.

I would not bother to tell this story, which I heard from

Klavdia Vasilyevna herself (it is ordinary enough, and volumes of similar tales could be collected if that were my purpose, for in the vast expanses of our motherland there is more than a little barbaric, medieval injustice). But the village of Ubory is hardly lost in the vast hinterland. It is half an hour from the capital, between two of the country's most exclusive sanatoria, "Sosny" and "Barvikha," which you cannot even approach without a pass, lest someone inadvertently disturb the peace of the Central Committee members staying there.

That would be the end of Kavdia Vasilyevna's tale, except for a certain fantastic incident. Kosygin himself happened to be staying at "Sosny." While taking a walk, he strayed outside the sanatorium grounds, and ended up at Ubory. There he met Klavdia Vasilyevna, who had just discovered the fraud. They got into conversation. ("I was with our old women, and he was with some other man.") Do you think she complained? It never entered her head. Modesty is one of the rural virtues. What did they talk about? Why, he asked them, why all the young people were so anxious to leave the countryside. He simply couldn't understand it, don't you know.

Custom is a bank of peasant needs, but a bank holding very limited capital. The peasant family may drink contaminated water for years without complaining or insisting on their rights to the ordinary amenities, because *everyone* drinks water like that. *Everyone* eats meat only on holidays. *No one* remembers a doctor paying a house call. What claims or necessities could there be?

The contemporary peasant occasionally listens to the radio, watches television, goes to the movies, and reads (or at least leafs through) the newspaper. But all the fine and just standards of daily living, morality and administration which reach him via these channels are just mere information. It would be impossible to follow them in everyday life.

Regardless of the abundant and varied diet of television characters — all those visitors to the "Russian *izba*" — the viewer has no way to get more food than usual, more than his neighbors, more or better food than what *everybody* eats. No matter how democratic the relationship between workers and management in the movies, everyone understands that this is just entertaining make-believe, and that in fact you do not approach the collective-farm director with your problems. He will not give you the time of day; he will be too busy; he will be hurrying to a committee meeting. Raise your voice in protest, and he will make mincemeat of you. No one can touch this confident economic planner, this district committee steward, as long as he fulfills the plan; at most he might be chided if he fails to shut up anyone who is dissatisfied. The dissatisfied person regards this mighty representative of state power as his enemy. Actually, it rarely reaches the point of enmity, except in the case of the truly desperate or despairing. Hostility of this kind ends, at best, with the peasant's forced repentance. At worst, the peasant has to bid farewell to his birthplace: approximately five percent of adults who leave the village are fleeing the anger of the authorities.[42] The director has the right to reduce the size of the individual plot; he can do a person out of his fair share of cattle feed; and he has

---

42. V.I. Staroverov, *Sotsial'no-demograficheskie problemy derevni* (Moscow, Nauka, 1975), p. 128.

many, many other ways of making a peasant's life impossible. But the peasant seldom violates custom, and to argue with management and insist on one's rights is, of course, contrary to custom.

Custom does not necessarily exploit its victim directly, as when our schoolteacher is forced to grow potatoes. More often, custom reveals itself in the activization or suppression of various needs. Urgent needs force the peasant to seek supplementary earnings. But where can he find them except on his own household parcel?

It is customary in the cucumber-growing village of Posady, where the machine-operator Tyukin lives, to build large stone houses. We already had the opportunity to admire the appearance of this village, with its glistening galvanized roofs. The houses are really not bad. One is particularly impressed by the enormous terraces, rare in peasant villages. Not every family can really afford such a terrace, not to mention the fact that they are utterly useless during ten months of the year. But houses are built, and will go on being built for a long time, in precisely that way. People knock themselves out searching for the colored glass that has disappeared from stores in the last few years, and deny themselves everything to build themselves a home like everyone else's.

Gavrya Tyukin might like something simpler, but he will not defy custom. After spending ten years of his life building a stone house with a galvanized roof with his own hands, he will go all out to add a terrace. But he will not improve the interior. Essentially, he will move out of an old, sour-smelling *izba* into another exactly like it, only more solid. This is not because Tyukin is afraid of the consequences of nonconformity — isolation and discomfort.

It is primarily because it is at least possible for him to build a terrace (even if it strains his resources), but he cannot manage running water, sewers or central heating. Custom may be despotic, but it is governed by economic realities. Custom may dictate a way of life, but the possibilities of living in one way or another establish custom itself.

Another researcher has acquainted us with the living arrangements of a machine-operator on the Karl Marx collective farm, which is located in a completely different region from Tyukin's, in the Orlov region, I believe.

> I wanted to build a new house — the old one was crowded and didn't have any conveniences. I saved up the money, spent five years getting together building materials, and at last I built it. It's not a bad house, as you can see. [The house has a slate roof and three rooms with high ceilings and large windows — interviewer's note.] It needed furnishing. Little by little we bought furniture, and we found just about everything we needed. Now we're saving up for a television set, plus I'd like to get a motor cycle.[43]

Vague and incomplete as it is, this interview gives us some idea of the difficulty the peasant has in building and acquiring the basic comforts of everyday life.

We know that the Posady peasants with their early cucumbers make two or three times as much as other

---

43. I.T. Levykin, *Teoreticheskie i metodologicheskie problemy sotsial'noy psikhologii (na opyte izucheniya psikhologii kolkhoznogo krest'yanstva)* (Moscow, Mysl', 1975), p. 85.

villages can make with potatoes. They live better than their neighbors. All the same, their standard of living (and also, evidently, that of the peasants in the Karl Marx collective farm) is barely above subsistence level. A large-screen television is about the summit of material and intellectual aspirations.

But there is another kind of life! There are "guiding lights" — we read about them in *Pravda* and *Ogonyok*, and look at the pictures. Farms do exist where the peasants receive more from the *kolkhoz* than many an industrial worker. Is material want less pressing on these farms, at least?

A certain writer (we know him already as the tender-hearted observer of the peasant's happiness without a horse), demonstrates the sociological approach. He was inspired this time to portray the daily life of what he regarded as a typical rural family. This was the family of a state-farm machine-operator with monthly earnings for two people of 484 rubles, which is twice the average. The writer notes enthusiastically: "The Aleksandrov family now generally spends twice as much money on manufactured goods as they did five or six years ago. A considerable amount has been spent on replacing old, outdated articles with new, up-to-date items. They broke up the old ottoman for firewood and bought a new sofa-bed in Leningrad, etc."[44] It is true: for a family that lived in utter poverty until recently, a family which even the author admits has only recently been able to get a cupboard, table and chairs,[45] even a sofa-bed is a luxury. May the Aleksandrovs sleep soundly on their

---

44. P. Shelest, *Odna sel'skeya sem'ya,* pp. 97, 75.
45. *Ibid.*

sofa-bed. But why all the excitement, dear colleague? You don't sleep on an ottoman, do you? And you must have had a table and chairs for more than a year.

Our Aksinya Egoryevna descirbed the progress in rural life more accurately than this publicist: "After the war and even not so long ago, you could walk down the street and see your neighbor scratching for lice. There were no curtains or trimmings on the windows. It's so much better now! Some people even have lace curtains."

Stylish furniture is far beyond the means of the vast majority of peasant families, whose income is half or a quarter that of the Aleksandrovs. If we measure the standard of living and demand of the peasant by the yardstick used for society as a whole we can dispense with the upper half of the scale. The television set, the triple wardrobe, and even the sofa-bed have made their way into some peasant homes. But the peasant's standard of living and level of demand essentially correspond to the poor, small-scale precapitalist economy which is the only kind possible on the personal plot, given the limited market, administrative restraints on large-scale individual initiative and the feudal relationships so characteristic of the society of "mature, developed socialism."

It comes as no surprise that "families whose individual plots account for a significant portion of the budget will not settle for smaller plots even if public facilities are offered" (apartments in large two- or three-storey apartment houses — L.T.). But, having admitted this obvious truth, investigators of living requirements are anxious to cover themselves: "There are groups of people in almost every village who prefer to live in two-storey buildings with all the conveniences and not engage in livestock raising or gardening, not have to heat the stove for the greater part of the year."[46] What does this sentence mean? Is there really anyone (for all the low level of peasant expectations) who *prefers* to heat the stove when, all else being equal, central heating is available? Is there anyone who enjoys digging his hands into cow dung, and would not *prefer* to stop doing it if he had the means, if he could buy machinery to replace the hand labor of the peasant, and if he could buy meat and milk? The peasant may drink "satisfactory" water all his life, but if there is a pure well — even at the end of the village — he will *prefer* it to any other.

The persistent surveys conducted by sociologists show that roughly 95% of collective farmers are satisfied with their material situation and work on the collective farm.[47] But in no way does it follow that, given the choice, they would not *prefer* a different way of life (and a different way of putting the questions on the part of the sociologists conducting the interview). But choice is precisely what they are not given.

It is not in "almost" every village, but in every village; not "groups of people," but the entire population, which *prefers* to live like human beings. There are only two ways in which this can come about. The peasant can become a hired laborer, a rural proletarian in the full sense of the word, receiving his share of the necessary product in the

---

46. *Migratsiya sel'skogo naseleniya*, p. 311.

47. See, for example, I.T. Levykin, "Agrarnye preobrazovaniya i izmeneniya psikhologii sovetskogo krest'yanstva," in *Problemy agrarnoy politiki KPSS na sovremennom etape* (Moscow, Politizdat, 1975), v. 2, p. 373. (Even authors of eulogies love to put the word "problem" in the titles of their articles and books, although it is not clear what kind of problems there can be if 95% of those questioned are satisfied with everything.)

form of wages. Or he can become a farmer, himself controlling the product of the farm, subject only to the laws and imperatives of the market. Under existing sociopolitical and economic conditions, neither alternative can be realized. Therefore, while continuing to *prefer* a civilized life with public utilities and the other blessings of our century, the peasant at the same time continues to heat the stove for the "greater part of the year" and to farm his personal plot. Unlike learned sociologists, the peasant tailors demands to reality. This is why he feeds both himself and the sociologists who study his preferences.

Chapter VII

In the last autumn of her life, Aksinya Egoryevna suddenly decided to call in the stove-setter and assemble a new Russian stove, because the dome had collapsed on the old one a long time ago, and there was a crack in the stoking-hole so large that mice were nesting in it. A little camphor stove had been heating the *izba* perfectly well for five years or more, but the defective stove was disturbing to the peace and harmony of her peasant soul. When a passing truck-driver stopped in the middle of the village street and offered to trade a load of sand for a bottle of vodka, Aksinya Egoryevna had the sand dumped next to her house and decided on the spot to procure a thousand bricks and call in the workman. But the stove did not get built in the fall, that kind of work is never done in winter, and by spring the mistress herself was no more. The broken stove occupied half the *izba* as before, but it no longer disturbed anyone's spiritual equilibrium.

In early April I was reminded of my neighbor's unfulfilled intent when the pile of sand suddenly emerged from beneath the snow between Aksinya Egoryevna's house and my own. I immediately forgot it again, though, and the sand became a playground for the children in our neighborhood.

I don't know how it came about, but country children — the Alyonushkas, Ivanushkas and Mashenkas of Russian fairy-tales — not only have different names nowadays, but also have given up on these fairy-tales in their games. In listening to the children's conversation and to their games on the sand lot, I have yet to hear a mention of fairy-tale beasts or mysterious powers. It may be, however, that children have always been pragmatic creatures, who prefer to play at being grown-ups, leaving it to the grown-ups to make up fairy-tales and play at being children? I don't know. The three-year-old daughter of some good friends of mine in Moscow always leaves an empty place beside her on the swing. It seems that this place is not really empty at all, because a house-fairy is sitting there. He is invisible to adults, but quite clear in her imagination — shaggy, kindly, and with a tooth-ache besides. This child has been brought up on fairy-tales.

But they did not play in house-spirits on the sand lot. A tiny red-haired girl of four, scarcely able to talk properly, used to repeat the same game day after day, much to the delight of herself and her playmate. She would take a child's milk can and pretend to go visit her mother at work, to get milk. The milk can would be filled with water or sand. "Now let's hide the milk," the little redhead would say. It took me a while to figure out that the children were playing at *stealing* milk from the farm, or rather, helping their mothers to steal milk (the mother of the readhead worked in the dairy). Children do not know the meaning of theft. For them, stealing milk is rather like playing "Hide the Thimble," but adults do not know what it means *not* to steal.

Recently, even in party circles, there has been more

and more talk of the colossal amount of theft in the country. They even cite some statistics and data gathered by the courts and law-enforcement agencies. But this does not begin to address the problem. In the first place, no numbers can convey the ubiquity of theft; secondly, the phenomenon has little to do with penal agencies. Theft, especially in the countryside, has become a matter of survival. It is a commercial line on the black market.

For the peasant, theft is the extension of his struggle for his share of the necessary product, the extension of **personal-plot farming. The peasant's work is impossible** without tools, without sheds, without thousands of small items: skeins of wire to mend the fence, machine oil to grease the wheels of the hand cart used to bring in the hay, the wheels themselves, nails. Hardly any of the many contraptions we gawk at in the peasant's yard has been purchased. This is not because the peasant is an innately immoral type and prefers to steal a dime's worth of nails rather than buy them. It is, simply, that there is no place to buy all that; none of these necessities are for sale. They are not for sale, but the farm must go on, which means that they are stolen.

Statistics do have their uses in making this clear: "In 1964, 37% less hay and straw was distributed on the average collective farm than in 1958. In certain regions public feed supplies were consequently plundered . . . In 1964 the losses in the Lvov and Nikolaev districts averaged, respectively, 85 and 150 kilograms of hay and 110 and 140 kilograms of straw for every peasant family."[48] This admission in print of the connection be-

---

48. G.V. Dyachkov, *Obshchestvennoe i lichnoe v kolkhozakh*, p. 57.

tween the production of an essential product and theft is unique. There is every reason to extend this connection to the personal-plot economy in general.

Who will sell the peasant the crucial two or three bags of fertilizer he needs? They will turn him down at the *kolkhoz*, claiming to be short themselves, and justly so. Thieves will sell it, though. But more often the peasant steals it himself; rural theft has not yet become a specialized occupation like the Tyukin family's cucumber business. The social division of labor has not penetrated very far into this trade, which can aptly be defined as "subsidiary and personal."

There is nothing in the stores except pails and shovels. But the collective farm has everything. If you need a cart-wheel, you go to the machine-shop, where you are likely to find some lying about. For a gatepost, go to a forester, who will pocket his cut and turn the other way when you take one from the forest. If you need the use of a vehicle to transport some firewood, do not bother asking the collective-farm director, for he will refuse. Make a deal with a driver — he will steal the service out of the *kolkoz* budget.

Where could Aksinya Egoryevna and Gavrya Tyukin have bought the load of sand they needed, one for repairing the stove, the other for building a house? Nowhere. But it is possible to arrange to have it stolen; the thief is paid in the same way Aksinya Egoryevna paid the driver. That driver, by the way, did not conduct his trade in sand secretly, at dead of night, but drove up in broad daylight and dumped a load of sand, and just as openly drove through the village soliciting orders for sand in exchange for vodka.

Nothing is available in the stores. Some things are not in stock, while others are not for sale at all. They cannot be ordered from the collective farm, which is itself short of supplies. Anything available for individual purchase goes first to the clique surrounding the director. Meanwhile, all around, people are buying and selling.

There is no legal market for the goods and services necessary to the peasant farm, but there is a flourishing market in stolen goods. If the fixed capital of the personal farming sector today is worth about 10 billion rubles, then each year theft in rural places must also run in the billions. Don't be misled by the Department of the Interior's absurd claim that annual theft in the whole country costs the government only two or three hundred million.[49]

Naturally, production materials are not the only objects of theft. If you steal the materials for building a shed, feed for the cow, and veterinary services, then why not go ahead and steal the final product — milk? And they do. They steal everything produced on the collective farm, except perhaps for livestock. However, they do connive in all sorts of ways to furtively slaughter the cattle and make off with the meat.

They steal, and they send their children to steal. I know large peasant families whose children begin stealing at the age of five. It is not the children who steal, I should say, but the adults who steal with children's hands. Suppose

49. *Ibid.* A moralistic position is out of place here. Moreover, this stolen goods market, which exists alongside the planned economy, amounts to something like a personal-plot economy for millions of urbanites. We shall have occasion to refer to this again, but, alas, a detailed investigation would lead us away from our main theme, the peasant's art of starving.

the whole family goes to the collective farm to work on the threshing floor, each one carrying a pail. The pay is not much, but just before leaving they moisten their buckets, and grain sticks to the wet sides. The smallest child has not been working, of course; he came along to play, but his elders see to it that his pockets are also stuffed with grain. Between the four or five people they collect half a pailful.

Women who work in the dairy teach the children to sneak milk away, even in children's cups. And the hot-water bottle is an ideal instrument for theft, perfect for stealing milk.

In the lean years after World War II they used to search the peasants returning from the fields. I found out about this by chance, when a woman I was talking with on the village street spat angrily after a man passing by. It turned out that he used to be the *kolkhoz* director, and had once searched her personally and found three carrots concealed in her clothing. She has been taking them home to her children. He took them away. These things are not forgotten even after thirty years.

But if adults steal as they work, that is, to acquire some product which they could not otherwise earn, children incur mainly a moral loss. The subsequent preaching of the Seventh Commandment in school will undermine the consistent worldview acquired through innocent childhood theft, but will it provide anything in return as solid as the conviction that stealing is the only means of survival?

Here it is appropriate to introduce some very important medical data which we omitted in the preceding chapter: "For the ages of 15 to 19, in rural districts compared with the city, a higher mortality rate is recorded from diseases of the nervous system of the sensory organs (2.5 times as many) and psychological breakdowns (3 times as many). Characteristically, in that age group not a single cause of death has higher indicators in the city than in rural districts."[50] Could it be that the heightened sensitivity of adolescence fatally exacerbates the obvious gap between reality and ideals propagated daily by all channels of information? Perhaps the delicate adolescent awareness perceives with tragic sagacity the lies which the small child still does not understand and to which the adult has become accustomed? There are, alas, no reliable data on this.

If every day a person must violate the accepted moral norms, if the propaganda he hears does not and cannot agree with the only possible mode of behavior, the words either lose their meaning or split the person's psyche, destroying his personality. This applies to the entire black market, as a matter of fact: everyone knows that bribery, speculation and theft are immoral, but no one can survive without bribes, specuflation and theft. The peasant knows perfectly well that theft is bad and immoral, but he goes on stealing. He continually hears that work is held sacred in Soviet society, but his work is treated as if it were *socially unprofitable*, as if society were charitably supporting an insolvent worker. Finally, the peasant always hears

50. M.S. Bednyy, *Prodolzhitel'nost' zhizni v gorodakh i selakh*, p. 46. In quoting, I took the liberty of correcting an obvious misprint. The actual text reads: "Characteristically, in this age-group not a single cause of death has lower indicators in the cities than in rural places." Obviously, the statement should read that in the cities those indicators are lower, which is clear from the numbers in the preceding sentence and from p. 43 of the pamphlet quoted.

about other people's splendid, happy lives, and sees them at the movies and on television, reads about them in newspapers and magazines. Recall the Aleksandrov family with their sofa-bed. He is overcome by cold misery, the dismal consciousness of being a *failure*.

The moral value of an ideology that juxtaposes a "radiant future" to the present life of society is doubtful to begin with. "When a generation is deprived of the possibility of freely disposing of its own property by being subordinated to the will of a generation long dead or to the rights of a generation yet to be born, that generation becomes incapable of actively contributing to the welfare of the country. It becomes in a certain sense disinterested, estranged from the land."[51] Sismondi's point is fully valid even in cases where the disposition of initiative and capital is artificially limited in favor of "planned, scientific production." The utopian ideas of a past generation and demagoguery purportedly for the sake of an unborn generation bring poverty and indifference to the generation of the present.

Of course, the peasant is not so simple-minded as to swallow this propaganda whole; he could not survive if that were the case. But neither is his consciousness so hardy that he can disregard the gulf between the general line and his own life. When it comes to social phenomena, causes have a way of turning out to be effects, but we can safely point to some kind of connection betwee the sense of inferiority and the pathologies of consciousness (nervous, psychological illnesses) and behavior (alcoholism, rudeness, hooliganism, rape).

---

51. Sismondi, *op. cit.*, p. 277.

No crime statistics are available, but experience shows that in a medium-sized village — about 150 to 200 households — at least one murder or other violent crime is committed each year. The population of an average village could easily be accommodated in a smallish city apartment building. Would city dwellers feel secure in a building where a murder is committed every year?

Let us not forget alcoholism and its sordid consequences: the bestial torpor of family life; the mentally-retarded children born to practically all rural families; the mutilation and ruined machinery; the arson; the murder; and, once again, the children whose lives are crippled by the atmosphere of drunkenness. This is the story, in short, of the degeneration of the people, the very people whom we prefer to regard as resistant to degeneracy.

There are no scholarly studies of drunkenness to be found. Alcoholism is not investigated systematically. Social planners do not recognize this topic; the planned society is moving towards communism, while degeneration takes place outside the plan.

There is no plan for degeneration as such, but a rigid plan of profitting from alcoholism does exist. The government takes advantage of everything, even the personal degradation of the alcoholic. We think that we can escape socialist reality by drinking. Think again! They catch up with us even here. The money we pay for vodka is nothing but an indirect tax. In restricted party stores, vodka is sold at cost; after all, party officials are not required to pay taxes. Experts claim — not in print, of course, but confidentially — that profits from the sale of vodka far exceed the current economic losses from alcoholism. The authorities will not readily give up this profit even if half the denizens of the victorious communist society will be idiots and congenital alcoholics. If the book sales quota in some rural district is not met, a carload of cheap vodka does the trick. It is the prime commodity in the official black market.

Chapter VIII

Constant shortages, strict prohibitions on individual initiative, and a government which cannot and will not satisfy basic human needs force us all, willy-nilly, onto the black market, where anything can be bought. The people are gouged for meat, clothing, building materials and other goods; the same people are squeezed for their labor, the labor of men, women, children and old people.

A man sees himself as a living token of the black market, and looks at others as black-market operators. These relations, though they hold together all of Soviet society, from top to bottom, are not studied by either sociologists or social psychologists. They emerge only in fiction, which is a more subtle instrument than the social sciences, and less constricted by governmental edicts. Here is how one writer describes a circle gathered around the dinner table, a scene which could be set in any Russian village:

> Pyotr Ivanovich wouldn't invite people of no account — he wasn't the sort to wine and dine just anybody. First of all come the big shots: the village council chairman and the director of the *kolkhoz*. Next comes the manager of the village store together with his

bookkeeper, and then the head of the timber station — that's because Pyotr Ivanovich's son works for him.

After that come lesser folk, such as the power-saw operator, the truck driver, and Antokha the stable-man. You couldn't take a step without them, the scoundrels. If you're roofing your house, you go and pay your respects to Arkasha the sawyer. Or take the stable-man. A useless man in our machine age, you say? But no, a driver is one thing, and a stable-man is another. When you need firewood or hay in winter, you address him as Anton Pavlovich, not Antokha. . .

Pyotr Ivanovich's guest of honor this evening was the school principal. Grigoriy Vasilyevich. The host fawned on him more than on the others. This was obviously because of Antonida. Antonida would work in the school, her path should be made smoother.

But Pelageya couldn't understand why Pyotr Ivanovich should be entertaining Afonka, the vet. Afonka was small fry now, since he was relieved of the post of party secretary last spring. They wrote about it in the district paper. When would he ever rise again?

Come now, how could the wise and observant Pelageya fail to grasp why Afonka the vet had been invited? Suppose he *were* to rise again? He was certain to do so, lest he drink himself into oblivion. And even if he had destroyed himself through drink, all was not lost. Influential friends would manage to prop him up.

Party secretaries, even former party secretaries, do not just come and go. Afonka is a consecrated figure. Yesterday he occupied a party post, and tomorrow will find him installed in some other position of authority. Although he may appear to be nothing but the servant of the big bosses on the district and regional committees and even higher, he is himself the boss like the chairmen of the *kolkhoz* and the village council. A small kingdom, but his own. He has his place in the ruling structure. On the black market he buys not only goods for himself and his family, but also cheap labor for the government. It is Afonka and his kind who help to rob the collective-farm peasants and force them to slave over their plots in their spare time.

What do we know about this new, previously unknown social structure, the party bureaucracy? Afonka is an atom of the state. Who personifies the idea of a socialist state? The party bureaucracy, the three million functionaries of the party apparatus and its agencies of propaganda and repression. They are the ruling structure, the preservers of the stability of the established sociopolitical and economic system. But as the idea outlives its usefulness and loses the people's trust, it also loses the dedication of the ruling structure. They no longer uphold the *idea*, but only their own power and personal privilege. The ruling structure presides over the black market less as an impersonal monitoring agency than as a trading partner with vital interests at stake. Who enjoys the greatest privilege under black-market conditions? Who benefits from the fact that any change, or thrust for change, is feared like the plague? Who, unable and unwilling to organize the country's economic life rationally, has the power to force the peasants and workers onto overtime? Who controls the greatest number of perks and benefits, which invariably surface as black-market commodities? Who metes out the cushiest jobs in the system (twentieth-century fiefs) and fills them with faithful Afonkas, deriving the utmost profit from the system? Finally, who can buy meat, shoes and books not through the back door and with a mark-up, but in their own stores at a discount? None other than professional politicians of all shapes and sizes, the party management who represent no one, but have all the fullness of power in the land.

All economic and political plans, all present governmental efforts are designed to preserve the political and material privileges of the party bureaucracy. That is the primary task; all other tasks, including the material and spiritual welfare of society, are of secondary importance in developing plans for the future.

The privileges are significantly greater than indicated by the comparison of monetary incomes — it is even difficult to measure them on the same scale.

The extremely low price of food in the special stores for party functionaries can be compared with the market price — for workers — but how can one compare their respective expenditures on food when the worker often cannot buy milk, meat and other vitally important products anywhere? The tiny rent which the party official pays **for housing can be compared with the peasant's huge** outlay to construct his own home, but how can one compare the luxurious apartments and villas for officials with **the overnight bunks in dormitories for workers and the** homeless, who number at least ten million (and even these accommodations are not enough, leading to intrigues, humiliations and bribes). Medical care is provided free to all, but a party bureaucrat registered at a special clinic gets a house call for a simple blood test, whereas a peasant with a broken arm will trudge miles to the nearest bus stop or hospital, or carry his sick child if need be. Even burial plots are doled out to the living rather than the dead. The higher your party rank, the finer the burial-ground, and your grave will not be washed away by the first spring floods, as happens in the carelessly built municipal cemeteries (municipal in name only, since, out of decency, they locate them as far as possible from the city, in districts full of dumping grounds and vegetable warehouses.)

In the world of secret exploitation and crooked economic machinations in which everyone is immersed regardless of personal will or desire, the party bureaucracy lords over the black market like underworld kingpins. The party post itself becomes a black-market commodity. Not people, but power-saws, trucks and horses sit at the tables of all the Pyotr Ivanoviches, with some minor party organizer or district council secretary at the head.

It would take a separate book to list party privileges in any detail. The book would reveal a social and economic system in which money earned has ceased to be a mark of social recognition, and become a blind, under the cover of which the ruling structure can arbitrarily confiscate goods. It would be highly interesting, but difficult to write such a book, because the economic boundaries of the ruling structure are very blurred. Its various strata participate to differing degrees in the appropriation and distribution of the surplus product. Some of the surplus product goes to research and development, which logically should lead to the creation of additional values and benefits for society. But in the socialist state the ruling structure naturally controls all technological development, and consequently funds projects which enhance its ruling position: the exact sciences pursue research connected with military production; social-science research facilitates the manipulation and stupefaction of the masses.

The technocratic class (people directly controlling production) and the scientific and artistic intelligentsia are all closely intertwined with the party bureaucracy. They all receive their share of the surplus product in proportion to their contribution to the system's stability as valued by the party bureaucracy, which is the only customer and patron of their work. Very curious are the benefits enjoyed by people at the lowest rungs of the party and government ladder, where the bureaucracy almost merges with the peasantry (or the peasantry extends up to the bureaucracy). These benefits and privileges concern, strangely enough, personal holdings. "The chairman of the Lautsesky village council (in the Latvian republic — L.T.) had on the collective farm a personal plot .97 hectare in size and, in addition, used one hectare of collective-farm clover to graze his own cattle. The chairman of the Prodsky village council appropriated for his personal use 2.11 hectares of collective-farm arable land."[52]

These two overplayed their hand and were taken to task. But specialists and administrative personnel on collective and state farms and village councils routinely

---

52. Dyachkov, *op. cit.,* p. 38.

exploit the farm's production funds to benefit their own individual holdings. "At the present time, administrators, especially those of lower asnd middle echelons, possess the largest personal plots."[53]

Leaving aside the extremes — top party leaders on the one hand, the Aksinya Egoryevnas and Tyukins on the other — one can speak of the greater or lesser privilege of various social strata and even of different geographical regions. The distribution of privileges depends entirely on the political goals of the party bureaucracy. Without a doubt, Moscow is the most privileged city in the country. The Muscovite works no harder than the worker in Odessa or Sverdlovsk, but his living conditions are superior in every way to those of the rest of the population. Considerations of prestige (before the West) are not the only reason for this. It provides a safeguard against discontent and agitation in the capital, which might influence the whole country.

For this reason, twice as much produce per person is sold in Moscow as in Odessa or Ashkhabad (547 rubles, as compared with 286 in Odessa and 270 in Ashkhabad).[54] One can conclude that residents of Odessa, who certainly have no personal plots, do not eat as well as Muscovites, even taking into account the hundreds of thousands of visitors who converge on Moscow to buy food (among them people from Odessa, although the two cities are 1526 kilometers apart). In other words, the worker from Odessa (or Kherson, Ryazan, Arkhangelsk) produces the same share of the product as his colleague in Moscow, but

---

53. G. Antonova, *K voprosu o perspektivakh sushchestvovaniya lichnogo podsobnogo khozyaystva naseleniya* (Moscow, 1975).

54. "O prodazhe i tsenakh na kolkhoznom rynke," (Moscow, 1975).

consumes far less. Because the ruling structure is less concerned about his political support, he and his family fall victim to the economic policies of the party bureaucracy. He is the first to be forced to sell his labor on the black market by working overtime, conducting business on the side or stealing.

The ruling structure arbitrarily sets the price for the economic system's most important commodity — labor. Social groups from whom it seeks political support are more highly rewarded. Thus, an extremely important truth: the more essential the role of one social group or another in supporting the rule of the party bureaucracy, the less its prosperity depends on failures and successes in the economy. The presence of commodities in the special stores does not depend on their availability in the country as a whole. Moscow shops are well stocked even in the leanest years, because the complacent prosperity of the capital is crucial for the system's stability.

The destiny of the rulers themselves does not depend in the least on economic circumstances. Economic failures in this or that branch of the economy rarely, if ever, affect the career of an official. As a rule, they are slightly reduced in rank or assigned to a similar position in a different line of work. Their removal is just a ritual to give the appearance of decisive action in the sphere of complete managerial irresponsibility.

No one is ultimately responsible for anything. No one looks beyond the last report sent off to the higher administration. When sociologists asked party and economic leaders for ther views concerning change (past and future) in rural areas, it was found that "of 545 replies, only 15 contain an overall evaluation of changes which have occurred, or are expected to occur . . . The small number of general evaluations of rural change suggests that management is more prone to analyze the concrete facts of rural life than to discuss the general question of the nature and depth of economic change in the countryside."[55]

They themselves have no conception of the mechanisms of privilege, of how goods end up in party stores or who pays for their perks. They neither know nor comprehend the society they govern. For instance, ninety percent of them believe that in a few years the personal-plot system will diminish or disappear entirely.[56] If that were to happen, what would they eat? That problem does not concern them; they know that as long as they have power, they will have plenty to eat.

Lack of responsibility seems to have become the main feature of the economic policy of the ruling class. Even a document as important as the Party Program promises that "within the next decade (1961-1970), the Soviet Union, in creating a material-technical basis for communism, will surpass the richest and most powerful capitalist country, the United States, in per-capita production. The material well-being and cultural-technological level of workers will improve significantly; everyone will be assured of prosperity; collective and state farms will become highly productive and profitable; the Soviet people's need for well-built housing will by and large be met; heavy manual labor will be abolished; the

---

55. R.V. Ryvkina, "Mneniya rukovoditeley sel'skogo khozyaystva o proisshedshikh izmeneniyakh derevni," in *Sovremennaya sibirskaya derevnya* (Novosibirsk, 1975), part 2, p. 92.

56. *Ibid.*, p 100.

USSR will have the shortest work day in the world."[57]

No one can be held to account for these promises, since no one is repsonsible for anything. On the black market that deals in party posts, qualities such as economic and political far-sightedness, talent and enterprise are not as much in demand as abject servility. Anyone who has this particular quality to offer need never fear financial ruin, regardless of the situation on the other, primary market where bread, cars, housing and labor circulate. Even a bad manager will be treated well by his superiors, as long as **he is a devoted servant, even to the extent of providing** him with a better-fief. A talented manager who is not loyal to the system will not last a day. Rather, his very talent will place him in opposition to the existing economic system, and he will be crushed, until he resigns himself to living by the law of mediocrity.

The Soviet system is a dictatorship of mediocrity, the dictatorship of mediocrity's TERROR of talent. It is this terror of free-market relationships, of *losing* on the market (a feeling with which we are all familiar) which sustains socialist ideas throughout the world. In our country, this overwhelming terror has become a governing force.

Talent is difficult to sift from mediocrity, of course, and there can be no question of a precise reckoning. We all possess a goodly amount of both qualities. The question is, which of them is more dispensable, which makes it easier to survive? Membership in the ruling structure is determined almost from childhood. Sociological research on education indicates that schoolchildren with no particular ability in mathematics, philology, biology

---

57. **Programma KPSS**, p. 65.

or other specialized disciplines are the most eager to "engage in social work," that is, to follow the instructions of their teachers and pioneer leaders.[58]

From among these pioneer activists are recruited the obedient Communist Youth League functionaries, who in turn become the party bureaucrats who control the fate of their erstwhile classmates, those with greater aptitude for mathematics, biology or management. Talent is made to serve mediocrity, and to live by its laws. Talent needs economic scope, freedom of enterprise, and democracy in order to be realized. Mediocrity has nothing to realize; the black market, the system of prohibitions, and the dictatorship of the party see to it that all is well.

Just as a peasant living off his individual plot can ignore the success or failure of production on the collective farm, a party official living off the black market in positions can afford to ignore the state of the economy as a whole. He has a personal plot of his own — the privileges and perks of office. He does not have to concern himself with the nitty-gritty of commerce. His job is to extract as much as possible for the state, and the state takes care of him. He keeps close watch on his own interests as well, of course.

No economic shock — neither economic failure nor the ruin of peasants and workers — appears to be capable of shaking the stability of the system, the security of party privileges. The fact that perks connected with party positions are allotted only in exchange for obedience and meekness (in the last analysis, for observing the prohibitions and suppressing all vitality and talent), regard-

---

58. *Sotsiologicheskie i ekonomicheskie problemy obrazovaniya* (Nauka, 1969).

less of economic results, is the strength of the ruling structure, but a serious weakness of the system as a whole. The feudal ways of the ruling structure, its economic backwardness and obtuseness, constantly inhibit the potential of industrial production, which under conditions of even relative freedom of market relations would provide a gigantic impulse to the development of the productive forces and signifiantly increase prosperity.

Chapter IX

It is simply astonishing how easily all the country's economic problems could be solved. Many believe — and this is the official position — that years and years are needed to "improve" agriculture, and that it requires a substantial investment of capital, technology, and personnel. The Dnepr Hydro had to be erected, now the Kama Automobile plant has to be built, and the Baikal-Amur railroad constructed. Nothing of the sort! All these complications are designed to conceal the truth: if collective and state farms were released from the severe administrative restrictions and prohibitions hampering their economic flexibility, the peasants themselves would "improve" agriculture, and their own lives along with it. Moreover, all these hydros, car plants, and railroads could be built more quickly and efficiently.

A few years ago, onions disappeared from the stores. The collective and state farms could not meet the demand. Several southern farms were permitted to rent land to some Koreans from Kazakhstan, experts in the cultivation of onions. The upshot was that the onion crop was enormously increased in one season. How simple!

Managers of our central-Russian farms, being short-handed, have begun importing (with official permission, of course) seasonal workers from the city, on the guarantee that they will receive a fairly high fixed percentage of the potatoes, vegetables and fruits harvested. The seasonal workers sell this produce in town at market prices. The work is lucrative enough to attract even well-paid urbanites. And wherever this system has taken hold, potatoes no longer perish under the snow, tomatoes no longer rot in the fields, and the apple crop is brought in intact. What could be simpler?

But why are only outsiders hired for such work? Why are they the only ones able to rent land? Do Koreans really grow onions so much better than Russian peasants? Is some Ph.D. really so much better at digging potatoes than a villager? I asked a certain sage collective-farm director in the Tula region about this. "If we rented land to the peasants, or gave them a quarter of the potato harvest, who would do his assigned work? What would happen to norms and wage-rates? Do you mean we should break up the collective farms? No, the educational atmosphere would be unfavorable."

We had completely forgotten that we were being educated!

Socialism is educating the new man, as they used to say, and still do. We shall see. But who comes closest to the ideal of the new man? Gavrya Tyukin and his wife, who wear themselves out on their garden plot after putting in a day's work on the collective farm? Or Afonka the vet and his friends, who are wholeheartedly devoted to every new district council secretary, even when he has them do the precise opposite of what they were doing the day before? Perhaps the ideal is Aksinya Egoryevna, all her life meekly feeding the officials who knowingly prevented her from living a normal life. They did not remove her picture from the Honor Board until after she died. Or Leonid Ilich Brezhnev himself — the perfect official who carries out orders and whose saintly life is now presented as our ideal.

We certainly are further from the socialist ideal than the party functionaries. They are uncertain of our dedication to socialist ideas, and reminders are posted on every pillar and wall (Work harder! Fulfill the five-year plan in four!), at work, on buses, in rest homes, everywhere. Even at the old folk's home, two or three of whose occupants are taken off to the morgue each morning, a sign near the entrance reads: "All-out for the Motherland!" Even in mental hospitals.

But no slogans adorn the austere corridors of the regional party committee, or the Central Committee headquarters, or the sanatoria where party leaders go to escape the daily grind. The gates of their suburban villas do not bear the inscription "A model housing project," as do the walls of the impoverished rural *izbas*. They do not bother with nonsense. They are not out to create the new man; everyone appointed to their ranks has automatically made it.

Do they sleep soundly behind the high walls of their suburban villas, take tranquil strolls, dine heartily on the finest foods from special stores, without giving a damn? Far from it. All these committees, commissions, resolutions! And why? All to produce two-thirds of the agricultural product from the ninety-eight percent of land directly under their control. They rush around, lie awake nights, drive down bad roads, come down hard with fist and boot, shout and drive themselves to despair in order to make people work conscientiously (that is, without pay) on that ninety-eight percent of land. And while they are working themselves up to fever pitch, glorifying socialist labor with the aid of slogans, banners and newspaper articles, people are quietly and calmly working on their minute parcels (the remaining two percent of land) and feeding half the population. Is it so difficult to comprehend the abundance that would result if the crippling prohibitions on personal initiative were removed?

It is, of course, not the peasant's moral welfare that concerns economic policy makers when the possibility of economic independence for the peasant is broached. A closer interest, the future of the party, is at stake. Economic independence threatens to turn into political independence.

In the late sixties, the era of liberal talk about economic reform, a madman named Ivan Nikiforovich Khudenko — may his name be remembered — persuaded some Soviet departments to try an experiment: to replace the innumerable bank accounts which not only finance the affairs of the collective farm, but control and regiment them as well, with a single account, and allow him as its chairman to decide how the money should be spent. The result was that the cost-price of grain was four times lower than anywhere else, profit per worker was seven times higher, and earnings four times higher than on other collective farms. Labor productivity tripled. Given our perpetual economic difficulties, one would think that Khudenko would become a national hero. But no: "We do not need every kind of increase of labor productivity." Khudenko died shortly thereafter, having been sentenced to three years in hard-labor camps.

His case provides a key to the essence of the government's economic policy. A participant in the affair published this account ten years ago:

"Four of us — all graduate design engineers — got together with I.N. Khudenko, the organizer and director of the experiment, and offered our services. I admit that it seemed difficult at first. As it turned out we were totally unaccustomed to making our own decisions, even though three of us had worked on major construction projects. What sort of houses should we build, and with what materials? How should we build them, what machines should come first? All this we began to decide for ourselves. After a while we acquired a taste for it, and began to feel like real managers, working for the common good.

I don't know how long ago . . . the neighboring sheep-rearing farm was built, but it still has no running water. It's been planned for five or six years, and the sheep-farm's spent heaps of money on contractors. Our construction team had been working less than a year in the settlement, and we had water merrily gurgling in the kitchen faucets and piped to all the units. We constructed a well and water tower ourselves in a few months, without blueprints or estimates. We don't need any estimates. You see, we don't have norms or tariffs or wage-rates, and we don't have to win anybody over: the lower the expenses, the higher everybody's earnings.

Along with an ordinary enterprise in Burunday that produced fodder we got imported units for making grass flour. The locals hadn't yet got them working, but we've had them going regularly since the middle of last year, and producing an excellent product. Again, it was because we didn't set up a special system for financing it, and we didn't hire a contractor. We jumped right in and assembled the units, got things going in the time it would have taken just to draw up the papers. We worked fast, but . . . we violated established procedure. Designers did the mechanical unit on overtime, outside the plan, though with permission from the authorities. Highly-qualified specialists also set up the automated equipment on their own time; we brought them out to the farm on weekends. And we paid them cash, as we'd agreed, not according to the norms or wage-scales, but as much as we thought was necessary. I don't deny that we overpaid the adjustors according to existing tariffs, but the factory works, you see.

Whenever we asked Khudenko whether we could do this or that, though it might be contrary to established procedures, he invariably replied: "Do whatever is expedient and useful, consistent with our own interests and those of the state. You may make mistakes, but that's not a capital offense."[59]

But it was a capital offense.

From the point of view of the defenders of the system, there was reason to kill. Khudenko had *broken open* the black market and let in the light and air of free-market relations. The whole fiscal mechanism of estimates, norms and wage-scales which Khudenko criminally avoided is set up to allow a significant portion of the product to be taken from the worker *without payment*, throwing him onto the black market. By means of this apparatus, the ruling class confiscates the necessary product from the peasant, forcing him to get it from the personal plot.

_____
59. *Literaturnaya gazeta*, Nov. 18, 1970.

This apparatus is safeguarded by a system of prohibitions and restrictions on management procedures. By giving the worker a direct material interest in the final result of his labor, Khudenko left no room in farming operations for the party bureaucracy. There was nothing to prohibit and no way to take anything away.

Khudenko's state farm was shielding itself from external administration. "We'll supply your grain and your grass flour. But away with your fiscal inspection, your police surveillance! Eat but keep your nose out of the kitchen!" Khudenko seemed to be saying.

If such an "experiment" were carried to conclusion, the administrative authorities could influence matters only by raising or lowering the prices of technology, materials, fertilizers . . . by engaging in commerce.

To become a trading partner means to let go of the **absolute privilege of power. To make a peasant into a trading partner means to give him breathing space, a sense of self-worth and the opportunity to develop civic awareness. But what if the latter should differ from the thought-pattern implanted by the party bureaucracy?**

A trading partner must strive everywhere and at every level to satisfy the material and spiritual needs of the people, must compete. But compete with whom? To become a trading partner means to take the risk of competition, of losing out to the competition. Considering the gallery of mediocrities admitted to the ruling structure over the years, such a loss is almost a foregone conclusion. Who would agree to such a fate? Khudenko was a naive dreamer, a sacrificial hero, to whom our descendants will no doubt do justice.

Are there no collective or state farms whose bank

accounts are in order, but whose labor productivity is almost as high as Khudenko's? Are there no isolated cases of productive farms that succeed within the bounds of the existing administrative order? There are. But do we properly understand where those bounds are located?

Behind the public economic life which is held up to view, with its flag ceremonies honoring top machine-operators, its gifts of lengths of cloth to dairymaids on March 8, the triple wardrobe belonging to the Aleksandrov family, lies another economic life, the secret, private world of the black market. How can we get more than our meager quota of building materials? Through bribery and speculation, as everybody knows. What enables us to obtain the spare parts for the motor pool? Bribery and speculation. Gas and oil are obtained, meat is processed, railway cars are found, timber, straw, the desired breed of cattle and a construction contractor all are located with the aid of bribery, speculation and corruption.

Everyone is well aware of the existence of this sphere of the economy; it touches each and every one of us in some way. Once in a while we get a closer view through the drunken dinner-table revelations of a director or his agents. But who today comprehends its general boundaries? Who discerns the dark underworld of economic illegality, secret economic machinations and hidden deceit behind the shining image of the model collective farm created by a photo-essay in *Ogonyok?*

Hidden from whom, incidentally? Only perhaps from us, the readers of the local and national press, to whom these collective farms are presented as the highest attainment of the *socialist* economy. But not from the district party committee. The party organs are well informed about black-market operations, if not in detail, then in principle. When necessary, they allow a restriction to be circumvented; when necessary, they look the other way. But as soon as the level of economic independence passes the "Khudenko mark," they crack down. They do not fear the black market. There is nothing so terrible about someone bending the rules with their consent, as long as he does not seek to revoke them altogether. Anything but an open market, economic and administrative independence. Under open-market conditions, the party bureaucracy would have no way of financing its state policy. The enormous funds which it can acquire in practically any quantity through a system of tariffs and norms, with the black market as a sphere of controlled initiatives, would vanish into thin air.

How does the black market differ from the open market? In the last analysis, in that the policy of the party **bureaucracy is financed through the mechanism of the** black market, while the mechanism of the open market primarily stimulates the development of the economy. The *black* market is a mechanism that supports the stability of the political system, its independence from economic laws. The *open* market is a mechanism that supports the stability of the economic system, its independence from the laws of political life. Either the market or socialism. Either economic stability or a stable political system independent of the welfare of society. Consequently all discussions of market socialism are an empty pastime. The more intelligent representatives of the government understand this. This is why the party bureaucracy will never allow land to be leased, as it was to the Koreans, on a large scale. This is why Khudenko's "experiment" was doomed and why there is more talk than action when it comes to unofficial pay for work on collective farms and construction crews, which would have real significance only at the Khudenko level of economic independence.

The more intelligent representatives of the government know full well that the socialist system cannot compete internationally with the open market. This was evident more than fifty years ago, at the height of NEP. It was precisely because of this clear failure that Stalin perceived what Lenin could not see: "We do not need every kind of increase of labor productivity."

Still, common sense fails to grasp why *every kind* cannot be utilized. Why three-, five- and ten-fold increases in production fail to impress the powers-that-be. We think everything has an explanation. All right, they have the power, let them keep it. No one is encroaching on their power. Only let us breathe, loosen the bonds. The more product there is, the greater their share, after all. Not all the higher-ups are like Abramov's character Afonka — some of them are intelligent, competent people. Why can't they understand? Why is it impossible to distinguish rationally between the free market which is totally rejected by socialism, and a free market for the benefit of socialism?

Common sense refuses to admit that the system has painted itself into a corner; it searches for an answer and, not wanting to accept the real reason, resorts to falsehoods. See, theft is to blame for it all — all thieves to the firing squad! But no, the dominance of the national minorities is to blame. Bureaucratization, red tape, sabotage, thickheaded senility are the cause. These judgments clutch at straws. Let them stay at the top, if only they'd slacken the bit. To think of change is frightening; change means blood! One should probe the extent to which market relations can be liberated under a socialist government. The answer is that they are as free as they will ever be — within the framework of the black market. The party bureaucracy's instinct of self-preservation, its knack for discerning political and economic sedition, can be trusted to prevent the process of liberation from proceeding further.

The Khudenko affair demonstrates the extent to which restrictions can be lifted; the "Khudenko line" is the limit of economic freedom under present conditions. Very few have gone that far, and no one has gone further. At least, we know of no one who has.

The Khudenko "experiment," which lasted only two years, brought the state over a million rubles in profit, but its organizer was convicted of failure to provide documents accounting for seven thousand rubles spent in running the farm. The charges were absurd. This happened despite the fact that "the ratio of management to labor on the experimental farm is 1 to 40, and on the neighboring farm 1 to 3.6"[60]

Ten times as efficient! Can our ruling structure really be interested in efficiency? This was the visible efficiency that threatened to shake the existing governmental order. By promising profits in the millions, Khudenko called into question the system of power.

The people who, in a fit of enthusiasm for reform, had sanctioned the "experiment," betrayed it at the last

---

60. *Ibid.*

minute. All the "intelligent," "broad-minded," "compe-tent" party workers, whom we mentally contrast to the drunken Afonka, turned their backs on the reform. We know that without party approval not a hair on the great manager's head would have been touched. They approved it. We know the man who first supported, and then betrayed Khudenko — Politburo member Kunaev. A judicial precedent was needed as a warning to others. They created one.

I have everywhere enclosed the word "experiment" in quotation marks, because what sort of experiment was it? It consisted of natural economic relationships verified by centuries of experience. The real historical experiment is what has been going on for more than sixty years in our country.

Chapter X

Socialism was once believed to be pure justice. From each according to his abilities, to each according to his work. Before we knew it, we had an enormous black market: you scratch my back, I'll scratch yours. Ability is wasted, work goes unrewarded and life is spent in pursuit of something to eat (even hundreds of miles away) and a few scraps of clothing. We see that a socialist country cannot be fed without forty million personal plots. We know that factories would stop for want of raw materials were it not for the skilled procurers, masters of bribery and speculation. The party apparatus itself, never mind procurers, could not function without fringe benefits — special stores, apartments and other privileges.

Is this the socialism of our dreams? Even party theorists now curse the simpleton who blurted without thinking: "The present generation of Soviet people will live under Communism!" All right, communism is easy enough to proclaim, but what will we eat under communism? As everyone knows, the planned growth rate of agricultural production in the last five-year period was only about 60 percent met. Will the future bring any improvement? The year 1976 saw a drop in the number of hogs. That same year, collective and state farms produced a million and a half tons less meat than in 1975. New Zealand lamb made its debut in Moscow stores in early 1977, and reappears periodically, thank goodness. In their 1979 annual report on the previous year's fulfillment of economic targets, the Central Statistical Administration omitted any reference to meat, milk or poultry — a bad sign.

Party officials are trying to compensate for the inherent defects of the system with familiar methods of administrative pressure. Some tens of thousands of meetings are held daily at various levels. It suffices to learn what is said at any one of them; the methods are the same everywhere. As chance would have it, I know verbatim from an eyewitness what was being said at a high level. Speaking in February, 1977, at a meeting of the secretaries of the regional committees of the party on agricultural problems, a member of the Politburo, one F. Kulakov (now deceased), claimed that he "would have the heads of those who do not show sufficient initiative in solving the problem." This peculiar understanding of initiative was expressed in connection with the diminished interest of some farms in planting buckwheat because purchase prices did not come close to justifying expenditures on that capricious and labor-intensive crop.

A few weeks later, the same statesman, at yet another meeting, declared literally: "We put the matter thus: You are not the secretary of the district committee if there are no vegetables in your district shops." Of course, as the idea moves from the Politburo level to that of the producer of the product, the managerial tone becomes harsher. Such is the feudal administrative style of economic policy. Unfortunately, at the very last link, the bureaucratic chain breaks! The peasant cannot be forced to work more than he is already working. So it is very doubtful that more vegetables and buckwheat meal will appear in the stores in the future. In any case, the appearance of buckwheat will signal the disappearance of, let us say, millet, or some other product whose production escaped for awhile the personal attention of the late Fyodor Davidovich Kulakov or his successor.

Ivan Nikiforovich Khudenko dreamed of making agricultural labor twenty times as productive, and he knew how to accomplish this. He knew how to organize things so that the five million people he proposed to leave in the countryside — or rather, who would remain there gladly, of their own free will — could feed the whole country. Everybody knows that the problem of production could be solved easily. But the educational atmosphere would be unfavorable.

What educational atmosphere? Who believes the slogans and visual propaganda? Education has nothing to do with it; the fact is that the *black market* might grow into an open one, in which the ruling structure would have less control over the final product.

No, we "do not need every kind of increase in labor productivity. We need a particular growth of labor productivity." And it is not so much labor productivity that we need, as the power of disposing of the product. State economic policy will not be determined by social demand. On the contrary, the policy of the ruling class will be to mold and compress social demand. Already the demand for meat is only half met, and meat is distributed in large industrial centers (Odessa, Rostov-on-

Don, and many others) strictly according to the work-place of the head of household, which amounts to a dis-guised rationing system.

Agricultural production averages 390 rubles a year per urban dweller, while 547 rubles worth is bought in Mos-cow; 415 rubles worth in Kiev and 286 rubles worth in Odessa; even less than that in Ryazan, Tambov, Perm. Odessa is the center of that southern Russian steppe which Sismondi said ought to, and Khudenko showed able to, flood the markets of Europe with cheap grain.[61]

The peasant has a personal plot where he can obtain the necessary product, but what of the industrial worker? He does the same thing. The industrial worker is more and more thrown onto the black market, where he sells his labor in order to eat and lead a normal life.

Pity the poor reader. It must be very tiresome to hear all about food, food, food, and nothing about the spirit; all about who eats what and who gets more and who gets less. After all, there is no famine, no catastrophe, no war! Everyone has enough to eat, no one is swollen from hunger, and there are not very many children suffering from rickets. How much of this hankering after someone else's share, looking into someone else's mouth, studying someone else's gluttony can a person be expected to take? The reader, rich or poor, is bound to cry a halt. Rich or poor, they agree that "man does not live by bread alone." The rich man declares it imperiously, the poor man shyly,

---

61. These materials were published in a special publication, *O prodazhe i tsenakh na kolkoznykh rynkakh*, (Moscow, 1975). I have already cited this pamphlet, but it is appropriate here to tell where it can be found: in the classified information collection of the Central Library of Agriculture. DSP no. 3762.

defending his human dignity, ashamed of his poverty. Poverty is humiliating, better not notice one's own poverty, it's an awfully bitter pill. "Let's change the subject!" they both say.

But this *is* another subject. This discussion is about the humiliation and corruption of the working man, who, even today, could make this a land of plenty. It is not our fault that discussion of the economy can never get beyond the theme of elementary need. Such is our life these days; we wonder where the next meal will come from.

In our time, workers should be able to create all the goods essential to society in an eight-hour day. Five or six hours day is enough for really demanding jobs. Forty hours a week. But we know that all Soviet workers stay overtime after the twentieth of every month, and every day during the last months of the year. We know that an enormous number of workers must look for work outside the factory or construction site. The construction worker moonlights fixing up apartments; the driver of a dumptruck delivers sand or gravel; his co-worker raises rabbits to sell at the market alongside the peasants.

Not only goods and services are sold, but also materials and tools stolen from the jobsite. Vehicles are temporarily borrowed from the workplace (a truck might be stolen for a couple of trips). And not everything goes on outside of working hours. Workers have learned how to pull the wool over the eyes of management, and they do their own work right there in the shop, on official time.

What alternative is there, when an industrial worker's take-home pay is 150 to 180 rubles, and meat costs 5 rubles a kilo at the market, potatoes cost 40 to 50 kopecks, and sauerkraut (this too has gone up since Aksinya

Egoryevna priced it) now costs a ruble a kilo on ordinary weekdays? It is no cheaper to shop in the stores, because outside of Moscow you cannot buy meat over the counter. There is a shortage. And if you pay the clerk under the counter, you end up spending as much as at the market. There may be plenty of potatoes in the stores, but two-thirds of the spuds are spoiled. Perhaps this is why peasant markets supplied 41 to 48% of the potatoes in Baku, Krasnodar, Armavir and Michurinsk; 66 to 77% in Dnepropetrovsk, Balashov and Odessa."[62]

It helps to have relatives living in the country: "Only twenty-one percent of families without personal plots but seventy percent of those with relatively large parcels help their relatives (living in the city — L.T.). No overall statistics are yet available on the contribution made by personal plots toward supplying the urban population with food (that is, mutual aid among relatives — L.T.), but rough estimates indicate that the volume of produce travelling this route is comparable to the amount sold at peasant markets."[63] But what if there are no relatives? What if the new city-dwellers were anxious to bring the old folks with them to town in order to qualify for extra living space? To buy everything at the market is out of the question.

An industrial or construction worker cannot earn enough to feed himself and his family by working eight hours a day at existing pay-rates: not enough to buy meat

---

62. *Ibid.*

63. T.P. Antonova, "K voprosu o vliyanii razmerov lichnykh podsobnykh khozyaystv na zanyatost' sel'skogo naseleniya, dosug i material'noe potreblenie," in *Sovremennaya sibirskaya derevnya*, part 1, p. 140. And this is all from that one-and-a-half to two percent of cultivated land!

through the back door, buy shoes from a speculator, and give bribes when necessary to obtain essential goods. Therefore, he has to work overtime at his job, or look for extra work on the side, or steal, or spend time growing vegetables in his own garden. He cannot survive without supplementing his regular "planned" work by selling his labor on the illicit black market. Neither could the professional politicians maintain the system's stability without purchasing "unplanned" black-market labor. (The concept of "planning" should not be taken as antithetical to the black market. All these black-market relations are also *planned*, but of course, this sort of *planning* is not likely to be publicized.)

How much would a worker have to be paid so as to be able to provide a normal life for himself and his family by working eight hours a day? Alas, we have no real understanding of labor costs in our country. Economists who have attempted to analyze labor as a commodity have repeatedly been attacked by the defenders of the official scientific canon. They have become almost the most common *negative* type in stories and novels.

Take the evidence of this recently published piece: "There is not one monograph that even attempts to analyze labor as an economic category — either in general or under socialist conditions — and to discover its material, as well as social, content. Many separate questions, which add up to the problem of labor, have remained unsolved. Many of them have scarcely been noted, and some have not even been formulated. One of the latter is the question of the peculiar characteristics of labor in an epoch of developed socialism. Scholarly work and textbooks have only one answer to this question:

labor has ceased to be a commodity. This is, of course, undeniable . . ."[64] Even this particular critic of Soviet political economy hides behind this "undeniable" postulate afraid of moving a step further.

Labor is a commodity. And those who are trying to get it more cheaply know this very well. Here is an example that indirectly reveals the attitude of the Soviet leadership towards labor value. It concerns the post-war reconstruction of the Zaporogh Steel Factory, a chapter in Brezhnev's biography. "At the time many thought it would be simpler and cheaper to tear down the remains, dismantle them and then build a new factory from the ground up. That is also what was recommended by the experts from UNRRA, an international organization dealing with aid to countries that had suffered from the Nazi invasion. After visiting Zaporogh, they unanimously agreed that it was impossible to repair the destruction, and that if such an experiment were attempted, more funds would be expended than if a brand-new factory were built. However, the country badly needed thin, cold-rolled sheet metal, of which Zaporogh Steel was to be the prime manufacturer, and so the Soviet people defied all the prognoses and predictions of foreign experts."[65] Wait a minute! What prognoses did they defy? Simply the question of cost was ignored. It was "necessary," even though the cost was prohibitive. Then again, what cost? Labor is well-nigh free, remember?

Foreign experts are often wrong in evaluating this or

---

64. B.L. Tsypin, *Rabochaya sila i ee osobennosti v period razvitogo sotsialisticheskogo obshchestva* (Moscow, 1978), p. 5.

65. *Leonid Ilich Brezhnev, Kratkiy biograficheskiy ocherk* (Moscow, 1976), p. 47.

that economic prospect in the Soviet Union. They assume a fixed cost of labor. But in practice, the cost of labor in the Soviet Union is valued very approximately and subjectively, depending on how the ruling class understands social necessity. The standard of living considered necessary for satisfying individual needs can in some cases be reduced to practically nothing, to labor-camp rations. The argument that "the country was in acute need" can be dismissed too. After the war, all countries were in need, and the restoration of the economy — for instance, in West Germany — went at an equally rapid pace, despite the fact that labor was far from being the cheapest commodity. Or perhaps because of that fact.

Not only in the years of post-war devastation, but to this very day the country's economic rulers, in their capacity as all-powerful sovereigns of the black market, force workers to sell their labor for a pittance, and to work significantly more than eight hours. Moreover, while appropriating the worker's overtime labor, these highly placed purchasers manage to imply that the workers worked badly for the prescribed eight hours and now have to make up for lost time to meet "the country's needs." This is done by means of the same quotas and purchase prices; for all their labor they receive what should be paid for an eight-hour work day. If they do not work overtime, they do not survive. All the accompanying slogans about the country's needs serve to obfuscate the issue. If the country's needs were really taken into account, the entire economy would be organized differently.

The productivity of unpaid labor refuses to increase. The worker's generosity is not inexhaustible. If labor is regularly exploited without a just return, men begin to work well below their potential. That is precisely what is happening in the Soviet Union, so much so that even party officials have noticed it: "Quite a few managers have pointed out that in the last ten to fifteen years the workers' attitude towards labor has changed. If statements critical of the technical-economic aspects of production are rare, criticism of the worker's attitude towards his work are much more common."[66] This feedback connection is perhaps the most prominant feature of current economic reality.

Today, there appears to be little difference between the lives of workers and peasants. But though it is possible to analyze the peasant's life, using data from the official Soviet press, no serious analysis of the worker's situation is possible. A witty Frenchman noted: "The working class has lost all individuality to the extent that of all the strata of the Soviet population, it is understood the least. We know the details of life in labor camps, but life in the factories remains almost a complete mystery." This applies not only to the French Sovietologist, but equally to those of us who live in city neighborhoods directly bordering on factories.

Statistics about overtime in industry and construction are nowhere to be found. This overtime itself is kept carefully hidden. I should think so! For the bureaucracy can somehow, indirectly concede that the peasantry has been sacrificed to the proletarian state, but what about the worker, the proletarian that supposedly rules the land? The fact that Soviet-style socialism is not the stuff of our

---

66. R.V. Ryvkina, "Mneniya rukovoditeley selskogo khozyaistva," p. 95.

dreams is not the point. The trouble is that the economic prospects are bleak. In his lengthy speeches to the plenums of the Central Committee on the subject of increasing the productivity of underpaid labor, Brezhnev never forgets to speak of the need for the peasants, and recently also the workers, to maintain their personal plots. But the workers' and collective farmers' individual plots, with their technology of remodeled mixers and vacuum cleaners, and their stolen construction materials, will not save agriculture. By betting on the further intensification of the personal-plot economy, the ruling structure is once again refusing to face the need for radical changes in the economy. The country does not need the "Association of Market-Gardeners and Horticulturists," but the development of an agricultural industry in which all socially necessary labor would be fully compensated.

A last farewell to Aksinya Egoryevna.

Her picture was removed from the Honor Board. She had worked her fill.

I looked after her house in April as best I could. I tried to drain the spring waters away from her cellar, and even went down there myself to see if anything was leaking. When the snow and the spring waters were past, I put up the wattle fence separating her garden from the street, which had collapsed. I kept expecting one of the daughters to come and sell the house or else plant the garden.

I don't know why, but an empty house is like an orphan. Whether because I did a bad job of putting up the fence, or because there were gaps somewhere, someone's hungry sheep, some ranging pigs, and a whole gaggle of noisy geese began to appear in the garden every day.

None of the relatives came, and I was already sadly envisioning the garden overgrown with weeds, the storage-shed collapsed, and little boys treading out paths in all directions. But everything turned out otherwise.

In mid-April I was visited by the herdsman of the collective farm. He lived just across the street, but we hardly knew each other. I knew only that he had eight children. I could always tell them from the other village children, but not from one another — they were all so red-haired and freckled, like their father.

"Are you claiming the plot?" — he asked.

"What plot?"

"Aksya's plot."

"No, I'm not."

"Then suppose I take it over," he remarked with an air of indifference. But the nonchalance disappeared as he walked away: "That land is awfully good. There used to be stables here — manure two meters deep. Aksya was lucky. Potatoes will do well here." And he departed, rejoicing in his own good fortune in acquiring such land.